Classroom Companion: Business

The Classroom Companion series in Business features foundational and introductory books aimed at students to learn the core concepts, fundamental methods, theories and tools of the subject. The books offer a firm foundation for students preparing to move towards advanced learning. Each book follows a clear didactic structure and presents easy adoption opportunities for lecturers.

More information about this series at http://link.springer.com/series/16374

Thomas A. Stetz

Test Bias in Employment Selection Testing

A Visual Introduction

Springer

Thomas A. Stetz
Hawaii Pacific University
Honolulu, HI
USA

Supplementary material of the book is available in springer.com

ISSN 2662-2866 ISSN 2662-2874 (electronic)
Classroom Companion: Business
ISBN 978-3-030-89924-0 ISBN 978-3-030-89925-7 (eBook)
https://doi.org/10.1007/978-3-030-89925-7

This Springer imprint is published by the registered company Springer Nature Switzerland AG
The registered company address is: Gewerbestrasse 11, 6330 Cham, Switzerland

Preface

In reviewing the literature on test bias, I have found two broad approaches. The first is highly technical. It involves complicated concepts and formulas and is only accessible and understandable by a few highly skilled individuals. The second approach attempts to discuss bias, but does so superficially and often does not approach the topic from a measurement perspective. This book aims to fill the gap between the two approaches. Some mathematics and statistics are involved, but computational and mathematical details are not dwelled upon. This book, instead, approaches test bias from a conceptual perspective. People are highly visual, and luckily, test bias lends itself nicely to graphs which are used a lot. Once you understand the basic concepts, you can move into other more complex topics and begin to understand the vast literature written about test bias. Unfortunately, most of it is inaccessible to those without a lot of testing or statistical knowledge and experience. However, do not let that stop you. The world always needs more statisticians and psychometricians. This simple book is the first step down that road.

Selection testing, hiring, and staffing are key competencies for human resource and other business professionals. Bringing on the right (or wrong) people can have long-term impact on any organization. Furthermore, hiring in a fair manner not only is important from a legal perspective, but a fair and legal employee selection leads directly into accurate and valid decisions. Even if there were no legal requirements to avoid test bias, any ethical person would still try to avoid biased testing. Unbiased test is not just important because of the law. It is important because it is the right thing to do.

Despite its importance, test bias is rarely covered in business, human resources, or psychology classes that directly, or indirectly, deal with testing. In fact, that is how this book came about. After teaching classes on organizational staffing to human resource students and tests and measurement classes to psychology students, I found myself preparing material on test bias. I have also worked in the field of human resources, communicating technical testing information to executives and human resource managers. My experience as an industrial and organizational psychologist working in human resources for over 22 years and teaching for over 12 years has allowed me to polish the material. Over the years, the class notes and briefings became more formalized and organized. They became more refined based on feedback and success of non-testing experts grasping the concepts. I firmly believe in the usefulness of having a solid understanding of test bias. I believe it will make students more employable and make professionals better users of tests, better users for test information, more influential in their organizations, and more effective in the selection functional area.

There are three target audiences for this book. First, human resource and staffing undergraduate and graduate classes. While employee selection is a core activity in human resources, its coverage is generally quite limited in textbooks and programs. This book was intentionally kept short, so it could serve as a supplemental text for a variety of classes.

Second, practicing human resource professionals would benefit from the book. Selection is a core activity in human resources, yet the technical aspects of it are poorly understood by practicing professionals. They must rely on outside expertise, industrial and organizational psychologists or other organizational consultants specializing in tests. Reading this book will make professionals better consumers of test information and better decision makers. Having this type of knowledge can also make human resource professionals more influential and effective in their organizations.

Third, psychology students will benefit from this book. A tests and measurement course in psychology degree programs is nearly a universal requirement. Unfortunately, test bias is almost never covered in introductory testing textbooks. While the examples in the book are geared toward employee selection, the principles are the same for all psychological tests.

I firmly believe in the importance of understanding bias from a psychometric measurement perspective. Having this knowledge will help students and professionals be better at their jobs. Given the huge life-altering impacts that testing can have on examinees, professionals owe it to them to be as knowledgeable as possible in all aspects of testing. This includes even difficult topics like bias. Buying this book (and even reading the preface!) is the first step. I look forward to guiding you to a better understanding of test bias.

Thomas A. Stetz
Honolulu, HI, USA

Contents

Introduction to Tests and Test Bias

Contents

T. A. Stetz, *Test Bias in Employment Selection Testing*, Classroom Companion: Business,
https://doi.org/10.1007/978-3-030-89925-7_1

Objectives

- Define tests.
- Describe why tests are used and provide examples.
- Compare and contrast test bias with test fairness.
- Explain the importance of test bias.
- Summarize the benefits of understanding tests and test bias.

One of the most influential documents ever written states, "We hold these truths to be self-evident, that all men are created equal ...." You don't have to have to be a US citizen to appreciate this statement. (We will ignore the dated gender-biased language, however.) Many diverse cultures, countries, and religions ascribe to this ideal.

In stark contrast, the entire purpose of testing is to differentiate among people. Thus, testing's basic assumption is that we are not all equal – in terms of what is being measured. If all people were equal, there would be no point of testing. Some people will necessarily get unfavorable test results. They may reflexively feel the test was unfair or biased. Because of this, many people are uncomfortable and fearful of testing. But it does not have to be this way. Knowledge is a great antidote to fear. Simply having a better understanding of tests and test bias can alleviate a lot of this uncomfortableness.

This book aims to educate non-psychometricians about tests and test bias. To do this, we need to first answer some basic questions. ▶ Chapter 1 answers the four following questions that will set the stage: (1) What are tests and why are they used? (2) What is bias and what is fairness? (3) Why do we seek to reduce bias? And (4) what can you expect to get out of this book?

1.1 What Are Tests and Why Are They Used?

Definitions of tests abound. There are differences among them, but the differences are minor and mostly wording. Below are examples from several authoritative sources.

The American Educational Research Association (AERA), the American Psychological Association (APA), and the National Council on Measurement in Education (NCME) are the three major professional organizations involved in testing. Jointly, they have issued highly respected standards regarding educational and psychological testing. In their most recent edition, they define a test as "a device or procedure in which a sample of an examinee's behavior in a specified domain is obtained and subsequently evaluated and scored using a standardized process" (AREA 2014, p. 2).

Another well-known set of testing guidelines issued by the APA seeks to provide psychologists with a set of best practices for using tests. These guidelines define tests as follows: "Psychological tests are defined as any psychometrically derived measurement instrument that assesses the psychological constructs in which a structured sample of an examinee's behavior in a specified domain is obtained and subsequently quantified, scored, interpreted, and synthesized using a standardized process for the purpose of evaluative conclusion or recommendation" (APA 2020, p. 5).

The Society for Industrial and Organizational Psychology (SIOP) is a professional organization that is heavily involved in employment selection testing. In their test validation standards, they define a test as any "specific processes or techniques by which domain-relevant information is elicited, collected, and subsequently used to make inferences" (SIOP 2018, p. 2).

Finally, well-known text book author and measurement expert Neil Salkind defines "a test as a (pick any of the following) tool, procedure, device, examination, investigation, assessment, or measure of an outcome (which is usually some kind of behavior)" (Salkind 2018, p. 8).

These definitions can inform our own understanding of what is a test. It is apparent that testing is a process or activity that involves three steps. First, behaviors are sampled or information collected. Second, what is gathered in the first step is evaluated, scored, or interpreted. (Some definitions exclude this, but I think it is implied.) And third, based on the score, some sort of inference or prediction is made or conclusion is drawn. This is illustrated in ◘ Fig. 1.1. Remember testing involves collecting, evaluating, and inferring.

After addressing what tests are, the next important question is, why do we use tests? The answer is very simple, because we want to make informed and accurate decisions. It has been long known that humans have many biases that can affect decisions and that decision makers are not always impartial. Tests are a way to reduce biases and increase impartiality. In fact, this has been known for so long that employment testing dates back over 2000 years. Civil service testing, to ensure qualified and capable government officials, began in China in the late Qin (Ch'in) or the early Han period around 200–100 B.C. (Bowman 1989).

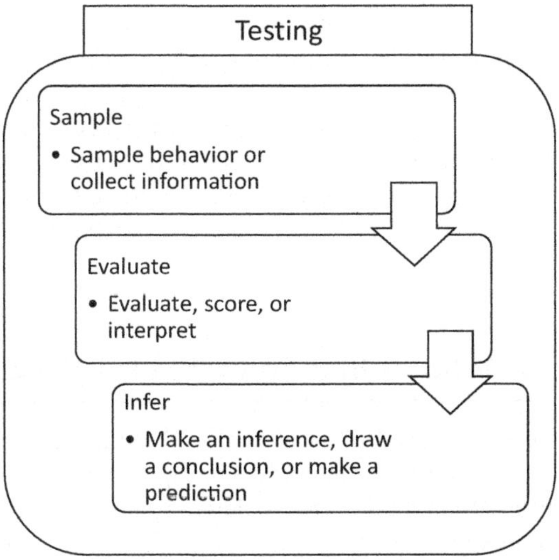

◘ **Fig. 1.1** The three activities of testing

A few examples will help to further illustrate what tests are, how they are used, and why they are used. During World War I, the Army had a large number of recruits. An efficient and effective method was needed to determine a person's capabilities and then place them in a position matching those capabilities. A group of psychologists lead by Robert Yerkes developed the Army Alpha test to assist with the war effort. This written test measured verbal ability, numerical ability, ability to follow directions, and knowledge of "common" information. Soon after developing the test, they realized that a large number of examines were either illiterate or non-English speakers. In response, they developed the nonverbal Army Beta test. All told, over 1.7 million men were administered the Army Alpha or Army Beta exam (Yoakum and Yerkes 1920).

Large-scale testing often occurs in educational settings. In 2020, over 2.2 million students took the SAT college entrance examination (College Board 2020). The SAT has two major components, math and evidence-based reading and writing sections. It is 3 hours long without an optional essay and 3 hours and 50 minutes long with the essay. It has been shown to be predictive of college success.

Tests, however, do not have to be large scale. There are many publicly available and propriety personality tests that can be used for a variety of purposes ranging from small-scale academic research projects to employee selection. The "Big Five" personality traits of openness, conscientiousness, agreeableness, extroversion, and neuroticism are broad measures that are often used. Despite personality tests having no "right" or "wrong" answers, they have been found to be related to job performance.

Further along the line of not having right or wrong answers are projective tests, such as the Rorschach inkblot test. This may surprise some people, but consider the three components of a test. First, an examinee is presented with inkblots and asked to say what comes to mind and to elaborate. Thus, behavior is sampled and information collected. Second, the replies are scored. There are standardized and systematic score procedures, such as the Exner system (Exner 2002). Finally, based on the scored results, a conclusion is drawn about the person.

In this book, we are particularly interested in testing that occurs in employment situations. For the most part, though, there is nothing special about employment testing. There are some legal issues selection testing experts need to be aware of, but the same logic, concepts, and analyses equally apply to nonemployment tests. Math and statistics work as well for educational testing, neuropsychological testing, diagnostic testing, or any other type of test done outside of an employment setting.

1.2 What Is Bias and What Is Fairness?

Testing is used in areas where there are many concerns other than pure measurement and psychometrics. Testing is rarely only about measurement. There are economic/budgetary issues, legal issues, social/societal issues, political issues, and philosophical issues that come into play when testing. As result, many diverse groups attempt to talk about testing. They, sadly, often talk past each other because they have fundamentally different approaches and concerns. They are really talking about different things. Such is the case with bias and fairness.

Fairness is a broad concept. It is a social concept rather than a technical one and, as a result, does not have a single technical definition (AERA, 2014; SIOP, 2018). One conceptualization of fairness is equal outcomes for all groups. Testing standards reject this view (AERA, 2014; SIOP, 2018). Different scores and outcomes for groups should raise scrutiny, but it does not mean there is bias. There can be, and often are, real differences among groups. Much more will be said about this throughout this book. Another view of fairness is equitable treatment of all examinees. All examines should have the same access to preparation materials, be tested under the same conditions, be given the same feedback, have the same opportunities to retake, etc. In addition, all examines should be treated similarly when making interpretations of test scores. Finally, the opposite of fairness, unfairness, can be the result of measurement bias. Thus, fairness is a wide-ranging concept, and lack of measurement bias is only one component of a fair test. Just because a person views a test as being unfair does not mean the test is biased in a technical measurement sense.

Unlike fairness, which is socially constructed, measurement bias is a technical concept. There are a number of technical definitions and approaches to uncovering bias. However, at a broad level "bias refers to systematic error in a test score that differentially affects the performance of different groups of test takers" (AERA, 2014, p. 23). Essentially, factors irrelevant to what is being measured is causing results in differences among groups. The remaining chapters cover several of the most common ways to uncover these measurement errors.

1.3 Why Do We Seek to Reduce Bias?

Because testing seeks to differentiate people, there is a common discomfort with testing. No one likes being told that their child may have a deficit or that he or she will not be hired. In addition, when test results are aggregated, differences among groups of examinees can appear. Testing then becomes an even more sensitive topic. Feelings and emotions can run high. Couple the emotionality of the topic with fundamentally different approaches, understandings, and goals, and this *hot topic* becomes difficult to discuss.

If testing in general is a hot topic, then test (and measurement) bias is a *white-hot topic*. A lot has been written from many perspectives concerning test bias. From a measurement perspective, test bias is pretty well understood, and there is an agreement surrounding many issues. Is there 100% agreement? Of course not. Psychologists, and highly technical psychometricians, debate fine details; after all, no one ever got tenure or made their name by agreeing with others. Such discussion is good because it leads to better measurement over time. However, it can also lead non-measurement experts to believe that there is no general consensus or agreement about test bias. This is simply not the case. Measurement experts argue about technical details but have broad agreement in many areas.

Remember the definition of bias in the last section. It is worth repeating here. Measurement "bias refers to systematic error in a test score that differentially affects the performance of different groups of test takers" (AERA, 2014, p. 23). Essentially, factors irrelevant to what is being measured cause errors, and this is referred to as measurement bias. This is bad because these irrelevant factors and resulting errors lower the accuracy of our inferences or conclusions. At a fundamental level, measurement error leads to unfairness because people are not being treated equally on the what is being measured. Instead, some other factor, extraneous to the test, is influencing the results and affecting our decisions. That is a lot to take in, and it is not expected that upon the first reading you will fully comprehend the implications of this last paragraph. By the end of this book, however, it should make more sense. In fact, I recommend that you mark this paragraph and reread it after you have completed the book.

Above describes why we seek to reduce bias from a purely technical perspective. However, there are also legal reasons that reduce bias. Use results from a biased test and the user can lose costly court cases. Biased tests are also more likely to be viewed unfavorably from examinees. As a result, they are more likely to file complaints and talk poorly about the organization. There are countless other reasons to be concerned about test bias and to work hard to reduce it. In the end, we seek to reduce test bias not because we have to (legally or for any other reason), but we do it because it is the right thing to do. We are making important decisions about people that affect their lives.

1.4 What Can You Expect to Get Out of This Book?

Measurement and psychometrics are highly technical endeavors that few completely understand. In this book, I will only scratch the surface of test bias. I explain the major approaches to test bias and what is commonly agreed upon by mainstream psychologists. I avoid overly technical language, mathematical details, and complicated formulas. Of course, some technical language and formulas are unavoidable, but I rely heavily on graphs to illustrate the most commonly accepted views of test bias.

In reviewing the literature on bias, I have found two broad approaches. The first is highly technical. It involves complicated formulas and is only accessible and understandable by a few highly skilled individuals. The second approach attempts to discuss bias but does so superficially. Most often it does not approach the topic from a measurement perspective. This book aims to fill the gap between the two approaches. I cover some mathematics and statistics, but I do not dwell on the computational and mathematical details. This book approaches test bias from a conceptual perspective. People are highly visual, and luckily test bias lends itself nicely to graphs and I will use a lot of them. Once you understand the basic concepts, you can move into other more complex topics and begin to understand the vast literature written about test bias. If you currently lack the technical testing and statistical knowledge, do not let that stop you. The world always needs more statisticians and psychometricians. This simple book could be the first step down that road.

This book will *not* make you a measurement expert nor will it give you the knowledge to perform test bias analyses on your own. It will, however, provide you with an understanding of the major approaches to test bias. This has several important benefits.

1. It will enable you to be a better consumer of test information, thereby allowing you to communicate more effectively with test developers and sellers. As a result, you can make better testing-related decisions and recommendations. The use of an invalid and/or biased test is not just wasteful but potentially harmful to organizations and examinees.
2. It will allow you to better communicate test results to test takers who are often anxious and concerned about their results. Understanding test bias from a psychometric perspective can improve your ability to effectively convey such information to them.
3. It will make you more influential and effective within your organization. Selection testing is a core human resources (HR) skill. However, in general, many HR practitioners lack in-depth knowledge. Having a solid understanding of selection issues gives you a leg up and leads to prestige among your colleagues and in the hierarchical chain of command.

After this introductory chapter, ► Chap. 2 presents the basic statistical ideas that are frequently used in the examination of test bias, in particular, linear regression. My approach is graphical and nonmathematical in nature, giving you enough information to apply the ideas to test bias but not overwhelm you with unnecessary details. Next, in ► Chap. 3, the most common approach to test, differential prediction, is presented. ► Chapter 4 builds on many of the ideas found in ► Chaps. 2 and 3. This chapter presents bias a function of measurement variance or how test items covary among themselves. Then follows ► Chap. 5, which presents differential item functioning. Again, this approach builds upon many ideas presented earlier. Finally, ► Chap. 6 covers the 4/5ths rule approach to test bias. This is not a psychometric approach to test bias, but it is the approach that has been included in US Federal selection testing guidelines and is therefore important to understand.

I firmly believe that once people understand bias from a psychometric measurement perspective, then an honest and open dialog about testing can occur. Remember, a lot of testing is not just about testing. Thus, before any intelligent discussion about bias and testing can occur, the participants must have at least an introductory knowledge of the technical aspects of measurement, psychometrics, and test bias.

1.5 Summary

In this chapter, testing and test bias were introduced. Tests involve three activities. First, a behavior is sampled. Second, the behavior is evaluated or scored. Third, an inference is drawn or a conclusion is made based on the evaluation. The concepts of fairness and bias were also introduced. Fairness is a broad social concept. In contrast, bias is a technical psychometric aspect of the test. For a test to be fair, it must be unbiased. However, an unbiased test, in a measurement sense, does not ensure that people will view the test as fair. Fairness encompasses a lot of other societal and philosophical considerations. Many people are fearful of tests and the potential unfavorable feedback that they may receive. This is understandable. However, learning about testing and test bias can help elevate these fears.

? Discussion Questions

1. Explain what are tests and why are tests used? Provide examples of several types of tests.
2. Obtain a popular (non-scholarly) and a scholarly definition for tests. How are they alike and how are the different? Are they consistent with the definitions presented in ► Chap. 1?
3. Compare and contrast test bias and test fairness.
4. Why is it important to understand test bias and why is it important to try to reduce test bias?
5. What are the benefits of having a better understanding of tests and test bias?

References

AERA, APA, & NCME. (2014). *Standards for educational and psychological testing*. American Educational Research Association.

APA. (2020). *APA guidelines for psychological assessment and evaluation*. American Psychological Association.

Bowman, M. L. (1989). Testing individual differences in ancient China. *American Psychologist, 44*, 576–578.

College Board (September 9, 2020). Nearly 2.2 million students in the class of 2020 took the SAT at least once. https://newsroom.collegeboard.org/nearly-22-million-students-class-2020-took-sat-least-once

Exner, J. E. (2002). *The Rorschach: Basic foundations and principles of interpretation: Volume 1*. John Wiley & Sons.

Salkind, N. J. (2018). *Tests & measurement for people who (think they) hate tests and measurement* (3rd ed.). Sage.

Society for Industrial and Organizational Psychology. (2018). *Principles for the validation and use of personnel selection procedures* (5th ed.). American Psychological Association.

Yoakum, C. S., & Yerkes, R. M. (1920). *Army mental tests*. Henry Holt and Company.

Linear Regression

Contents

T. A. Stetz, *Test Bias in Employment Selection Testing*, Classroom Companion: Business,
https://doi.org/10.1007/978-3-030-89925-7_2

2

Objectives

- Understand fundamental graphing concepts used in linear regression and test bias analysis.
- Explain how linear regression finds the best fitting line and why this is important.
- Know the mathematical equation for a straight line and what each component represents.
- Describe predictive validity and apply the concept to identify likely successful and unsuccessful new hires.

To truly understand measurement bias, you must understand some basic math, statistics, and psychometrics. There will be some formulas, but math is really more about thinking. Once you understand the basic concepts, we can apply them to various testing situations. Fully thinking through the implications when the concepts are applied to testing situations is actually harder than the math or statistics part. This chapter explains some of the basic statistical ideas that will be used throughout the book.

2.1 Graphing and Plotting Test Scores

We will use one testing scenario for most of the examples that follow in this chapter. In our scenario, we give a test to newly hired employees right before they start working. Then 6 months later, we measure their job performance.

In everyday use, the words "graph" and "plot" are used interchangeably. However, there are slight differences in what each word means. I believe that a discussion of the differences is irrelevant to what we are trying to accomplish here. It is just mentioned for the sticklers out there. I am simply using the word graph to describe a visual representation of data.

The usefulness of a test is generally indicated by the relationship between test score and job performance. This is called *predictive validity*. Because we are examining two variables at the same time, we set up a graph with two axes – one for test score and one for job performance. Using the conventional graphing approaches, we place test score on the horizontal axis and job performance on the vertical axis. This setup indicates that we are predicting job performance from test score. The predictor generally goes on the horizontal axis and the outcome on the vertical axis. As we move from left to right, test scores increase. As we go from bottom to top, job performance increases. ◘ Figure 2.1 illustrates this basic graphing setup.

If you spend any time reading about test bias, you will come across the words *predictor* and *criterion*. The word predictor is pretty easily understood. In this case, we are using a test score to predict something, so it is the predictor variable. The word criterion is less intuitive, but it is a simple concept. Criterion is just a fancy way to refer to the outcome in which we are interested. In other words, the criterion is what we wish to predict. In this case, it is job performance. Thus, predictors pre-

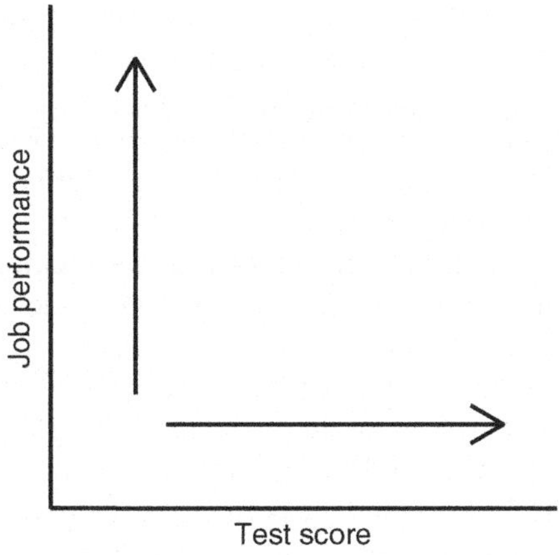

■ **Fig. 2.1** Basic graphing area layout

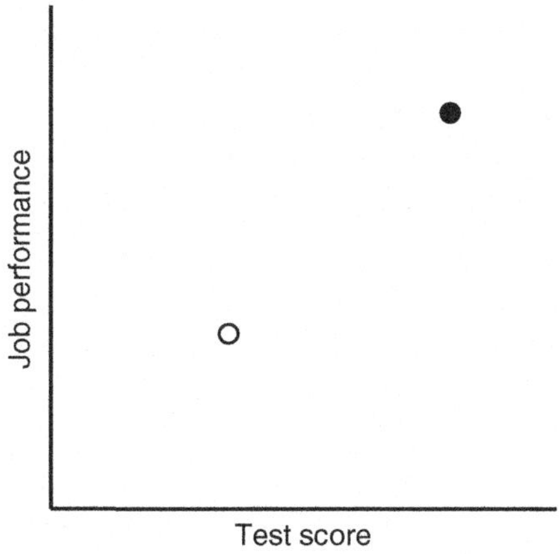

■ **Fig. 2.2** Example of graph with two individuals

dict criterions. In our example, test scores are used to predict job performance. This is shown below.

$$\text{Predictor} \rightarrow \text{Criterion}$$

$$\text{Test score} \rightarrow \text{Job performance}$$

For a test to be valid, we expect that individuals who score high on the test will also have high job performance. We would likewise expect that individuals who score low on the test would also have low job performance. This is what is meant by *predictive validity*. The graph in ■ Fig. 2.2 shows that two people took the test and were evaluated on job performance. These two individuals are represented by the white and grey dots. Looking at the graph, you can see that the grey individual scored high on the test and also had high job performance. In contrast, the white individual scored low on the test and subsequently had low job performance. In a real test situation, there are many more pairs of scores plotted on the graph.

Now suppose we gave the test and later evaluated job performance for 40 new hires. We plotted each person's test score against his or her job performance. If the test is valid, the graph would look something like this graph shown in ◻ Fig. 2.3. You can see that there is a general pattern. Higher test scores tend to be associated with higher job performance. Notice that I used the words "general" and "tend." No test is perfect.

This next graph, ◻ Fig. 2.4, demonstrates several more important points. First look at the white circle and the circle-plus. These are the two highest test scores. We know this because test scores go from low to high (left to right); the two scores farthest to the right are the highest on the test. In this example, the individual represented by circle-plus had higher job performance than the individual represented by white circle, even though they have the exact same test score. This is okay and is to be expected. A perfect test or perfect measurement is an ideal that can never be achieved, not in the psychological sciences, medicine, or even physics. We could debate about how much difference in job performance is acceptable when people have the same test score, but that is an entirely different discussion.

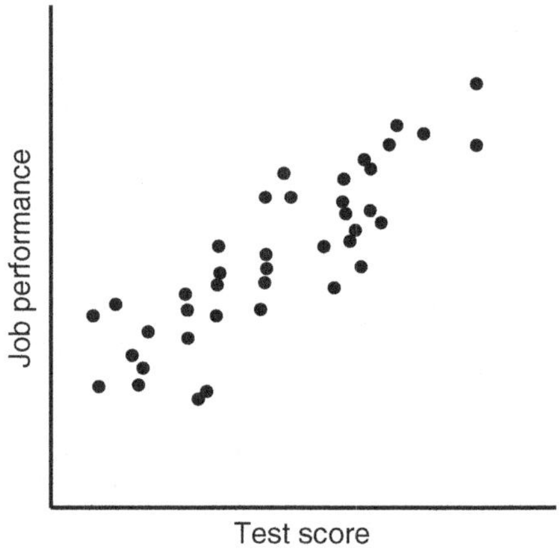

◻ **Fig. 2.3** Graph of test score and job performance for 40 individuals

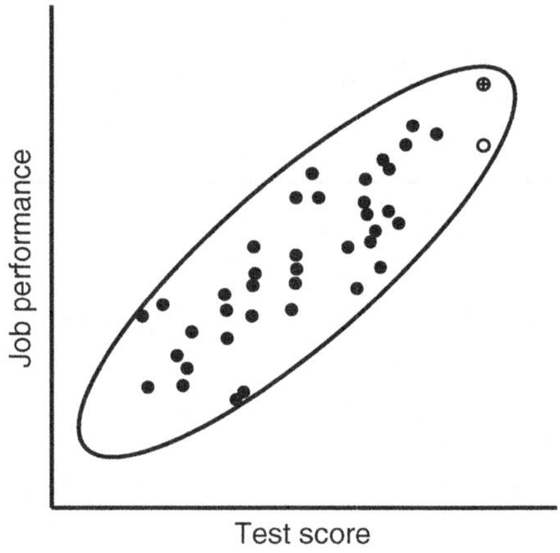

◻ **Fig. 2.4** Graph illustrating that two individuals can have the same test score, but different levels of job performance

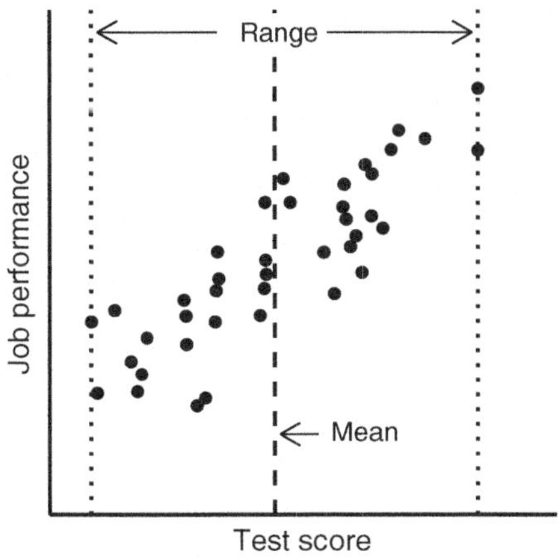

Fig. 2.5 Graph illustrating the range and mean of test scores

Surely you noticed the oval around the dots. Sometimes measurement experts do this to save time. It is easier to draw one oval than it is to plot 40 points for pairs of test score and job performance. In the future, if you ever see an oval on a graph, just understand that it represents a bunch of test scores plotted against job performance, and the general shape is like the oval. We do not need to know every single pair of scores because we are looking for general patterns in the data.

The next two graphs illustrate two other important concepts. The first concept is that of the mean, which is commonly called the average. The second concept is the range, which concerns the entire spread of scores. Figure 2.5 shows these concepts for test scores. Test scores go from left to right or low to high. The left and right dotted lines show the low- and high-test scores, respectively. Ignore the vertical displacement of the dots because that shows you job performance. You could imagine all the dots at the bottom, top, middle, etc. It does not matter. Right now, we only care about test score, which is horizontal left to right. If we wanted to cut the distribution of test scores in half right down the middle, we would draw a line in the middle of the range. The center dashed line does this and represents the mean test score.

In Fig. 2.6, these concepts are illustrated for job performance. We just rotate our perspective. Job performance falls along the vertical y-axis. Job performance goes from low to high (bottom to top). The bottom and top dotted lines show the range of job performance, and the center dashed line shows the mean or average job performance of everyone who took the test. Make sure you understand these concepts because they will be important later.

2.2 Linear Regression Visually

We now move on to linear regression. A lot has been written about linear regression, but I will stick to the absolute bare minimum. Very simply, this approach shows the degree of association between two variables. In our example, the two variables are test score and job performance. The technique draws the "best fitting"

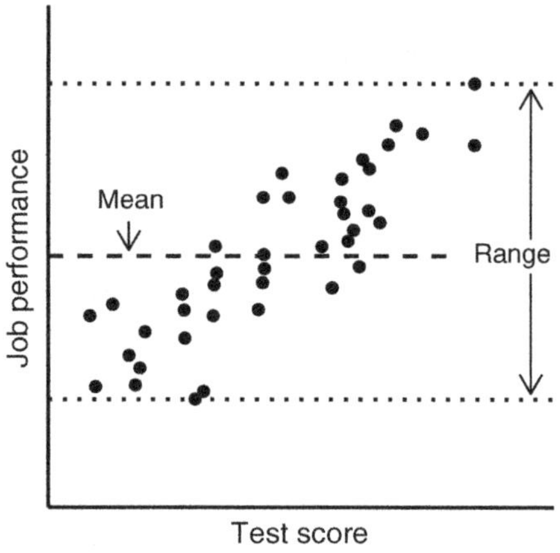

Fig. 2.6 Graph illustrating range and mean of job performance

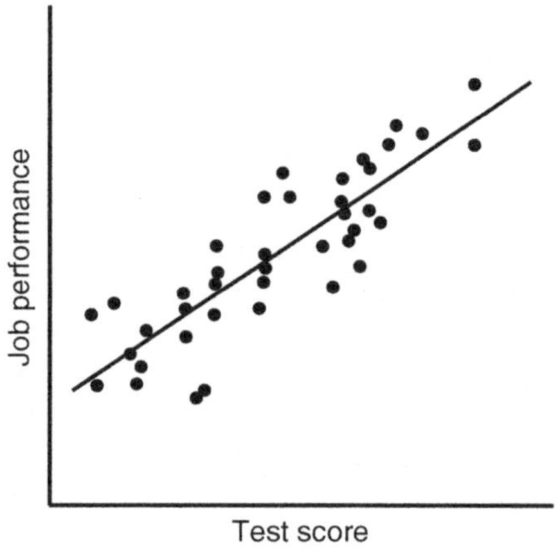

Fig. 2.7 Graph showing the best fitting line through data points

line through the data points on the graph. Linear regression is as simple as that. The graph in Fig. 2.7 shows the best fitting line through the data we have been working with.

Now assume that we have a second test. We also gave this test to the new hires at the same. The graph below shows the relationship between test score and job performance for this second test. If you compare the graphs in Fig. 2.8 and to Fig. 2.7, you will notice that the best fitting lines look quite different. In Fig. 2.7, the best fitting line is fairly steep. This shows that as test scores increase, so does job performance. In Fig. 2.8, the line is very flat. Thus, as test scores increase, job performance does not change much. This difference has important testing implications.

When making decisions based on a test, we would prefer to have a graph more like the one shown in Fig. 2.7 than the one in Fig. 2.8. The reason is that in Fig. 2.7, we know that a high scoring person will likely perform much better on the job than a low scoring person. In contrast, when the line is flat, a high scoring person will not perform on the job much better, if at all, than a low scoring person.

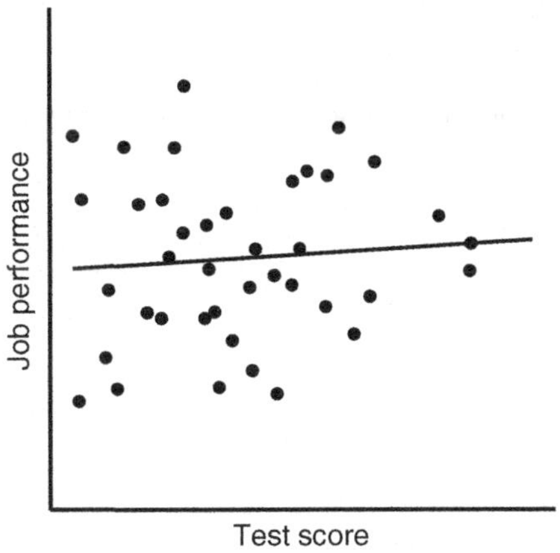

Fig. 2.8 Graph showing the best fitting line when there is little association between test score and job performance

Therefore, a flat line does not help us predict who will perform well on the job. We want steep lines.

2.3 Linear Regression Mathematically

This next section provides a more mathematically explanation of linear regression. Readers are encouraged to thoroughly go through this section. It will provide for a deeper understanding of regression and subsequently test bias. However, it is not strictly needed to understand the test bias concepts that will be presented in later chapters.

In the previous section, it was stated that regression finds the "best fitting" line between the points. What does that mean? While there are various kinds of regression, the most common is *ordinary least squares* regression. In this type, the best fitting (straight) line minimizes the vertical distance between the line and all of the points in the scatterplot. We could, of course, fit many different straight lines through the points. However, there is only one line that will minimize the vertical differences between the points and line. For any other line, this difference will be larger.

Figure 2.9 gives an example with four test scores. The best fitting line in ordinary least squares regression minimizes the distance between the points and the line, and this distance is represented by the dashed vertical lines. (Technically, for mathematical reasons, regression minimizes the squared difference between the point and the line. Readers who are interested in why this is should refer to any introductory statistics textbook, which will provide a full explanation.)

Some readers may wonder why do we care about the vertical error and not the horizontal error. Remember that the predictor variable goes on the horizontal axis and the criterion variable on the vertical axis. We want to be as accurate as possible in our predictions of the criterion, and this requires minimizing the vertical error. If you find the vertical distance each point is from the line, sum this, and then divide by the total number of points, we get an average. This is the average distance

2

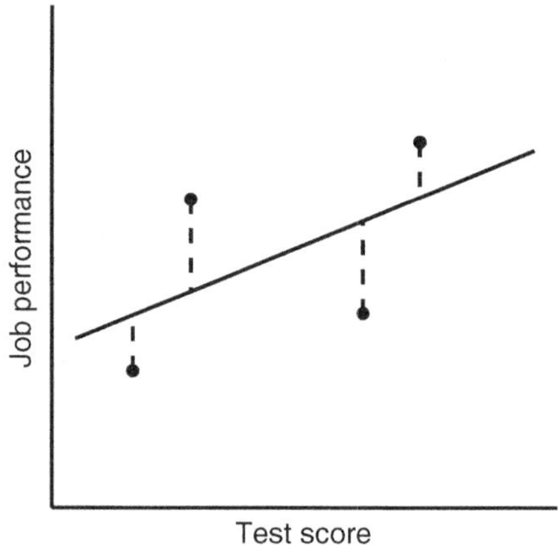

Fig. 2.9 Graph illustrating how the best fitting line minimizes the distance between the line and actual job performance

that we are wrong in our predictions using our regression line. This is called the *standard error of estimate*, and it helps us know how good predictions are. The best fitting line will always minimize the standard error of estimate, ensuring that our prediction is as accurate as possible with the information that we have.

Mostly likely from your high school math class, you were told the equation for a straight line.

$$y = mx + b$$

It is the same in regression, but different symbols tend to be used. There is no single standard convention, but it is generally written similarly to the formula below.

$$Y' = bX + a$$

These two equations look similar and that is because they are the same equation. In statistics, often times different letters or symbols are used to convey the same thing.

- Y' is the value we are trying to predict (the criterion value in this case job performance).
- b is the slope of the line.
- X is the value of x that we are using to predict Y' (in this case, x is a test score).
- a is the point where the line crosses the y-axis (in this case, the job performance axis).

2.4 Predictive Validity

Our current scenario works fine to understand the relationship between test score and job performance for our 40 new hires. The best fitting linear regression line shows that individuals who score higher on the test have higher job performance. Thus, we can say that the test is valid for its intended use in predicting job performance. Putting it in another way, the test has *predictive validity*. That is a good first step. However, our real goal is to be able to use the test to hire the best applicants. Luckily, regression allows us to do that.

The graph we have been working with is based on the people that we have already hired and who have been working for us for 6 months. When we hire new people, we will not know their job performance until 6 months later. However, we can use the information in the graph to predict if a new applicant will be successful or unsuccessful on the job.

At this point, I am going to add another piece of information to our main graph. Because the graph has job performance on the *y*-axis, it is easy to distinguish between successful and unsuccessful employees. All we have to do is draw a line on the scale at the "unsuccessful" rating point. Thus, I will add a dashed horizontal line that shows the *unsuccessful* cut point on our job performance axis. Any person who is below this line is unsuccessful. Anyone above it is successful on the job.

Remember that when hiring a new applicant, the only information we will have is their test score. Therefore, we have to associate this job performance cut point to the test scores. To do this, I look for where our cut point touches the regression line and draw a vertical line. This is because this is our best guess at relating unsuccessful job performance to a test score. The vertical line determines what score the person must obtain for us to predict that he or she will be a successful employee. All of this is shown in ◘ Fig. 2.10.

These two dashed lines cut our graph into four quadrants. All of the points in the upper right quadrant are correct decisions. Based on the test score, we would predict that these people would be successful. Based on their later job performance ratings, they are. The points in the lower left quadrant are also correct decisions. Based on their test scores, we would predict them to be unsuccessful, and their later job performance ratings show that they are indeed unsuccessful.

We also have incorrect decisions. Look at the lower right quadrant. Using the information available at hiring time, we predict that they would be successful. However, they fall below the horizontal job performance line, and therefore when we measured their performance later, we found them unsuccessful. The points in

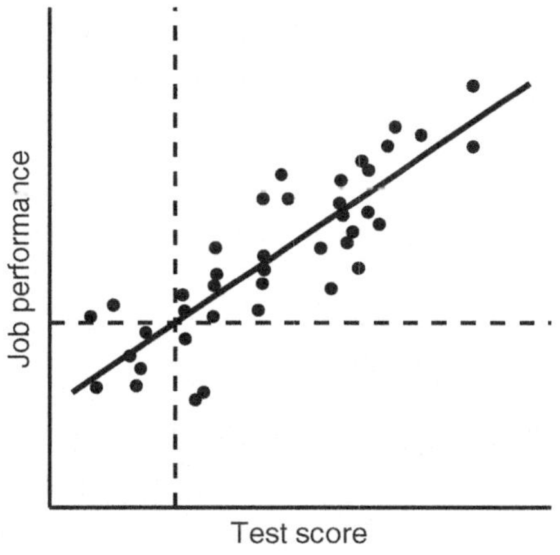

◘ **Fig. 2.10** Graph of test score and job performance with the best fitting line and cut points for test score and job performance

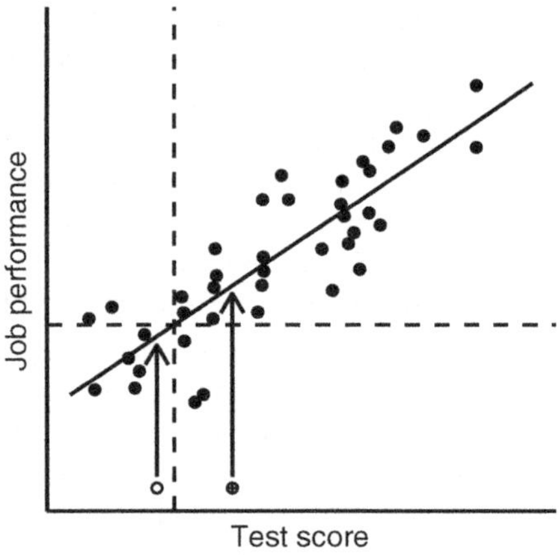

Fig. 2.11 Graph showing how job performance can be predicted for two new test takers

the upper left quadrant are also incorrect decisions. Based on the test score, we would predict that they would be unsuccessful, but their later job performance ratings show that they are above the job performance cut point and, therefore, are successful employees. The goal is to get as many of the dots in the upper right and lower left quadrants as these are correct decisions. Likewise, we want to minimize the number of dots in the upper left and lower right quadrants as these are incorrect decisions. All of this is shown in Fig. 2.10.

Using the information in the graph, we can determine how accurate we are in our decisions in our past decisions and, therefore, how accurate we are likely to be in our future decisions. We know we hired 40 people and five of them fall in the incorrect decision quadrants of Fig. 2.10. Based on all of the information we have, we can project that when the test is used about 12.5% of our decisions will be incorrect (5/40 = 0.125) and about 87.5% of our decisions will be incorrect (35/40 = 0.875).

Suppose we need to hire two more employees. We give the test to the two new applicants. At this point, we do not know their job performance. We only know their test score. However, we can predict their job performance with our regression line. Because we only know their test scores in Fig. 2.11, I put a point at their test scores along the x-axis. If we go straight up to the regression line, this is what we predict their job performance will be. We can see that the white circle applicant will likely be unsuccessful on the job while the circle-plus applicant will likely succeed. Therefore, we probably should not hire white circle and wait for another better performing employee. The circle-plus applicant will not be an outstanding employee but will likely be acceptable.

2.5 Summary

This chapter is a gentle introduction into the main concepts that play into the analysis of test bias. It is important to keep in mind that test bias is a technical and mathematical endeavor. Any true understanding of it requires an understanding of some mathematical concepts. While the underlying math may be complicated at times, conceptually it is more straightforward.

When it comes to testing, we are particularly concerned about a test's predictive validity. That is the ability for a test to predict some outcome (called a criterion). This prediction should be as accurate as possible. We can assess a test's prediction accuracy using regression analysis.

In the next chapter, we will further discuss how regression analysis and how it can be used to compare the performance for different groups of people. This is the key to understanding test bias.

Discussion Questions

1. This chapter presents how to use linear regression to predict job performance from test scores. Discuss other situations when linear regression could be used. Be sure to address what is the predictor and what is the criterion, what sort of graph you would construct, and what you would expect the graph would look like.
2. Fully explain how linear regression finds the best fitting line.
3. What is meant by predictive validity? Explain the concept and provide an illustrative example.
4. When using linear regression to predict job performance from test scores, explain why you would want the linear regression line to be steep rather than flat.
5. Construct a graph showing a set of test scores and job performance ratings. Draw a vertical line representing a test cut score and a horizontal line representing a minimum acceptable job performance, so the graph is cut into four quadrants. Explain what each quadrant means in terms of selection decisions.

Differential Test Prediction

Contents

T. A. Stetz, *Test Bias in Employment Selection Testing*, Classroom Companion: Business,
https://doi.org/10.1007/978-3-030-89925-7_3

Objectives

- Describe the basic process of detecting differential prediction using regression lines.
- Explain why group differences in test scores does not necessarily mean the test is bias.
- Identify the various ways in which differential test prediction can occur.
- Discuss the implications of the 1991 Civil Rights Act and its impact on over- and underprediction for the majority and minority groups.

With the preliminaries out of the way, we can begin to explore test bias. This chapter will present a specific type of test bias called *differential test prediction*. I will use the same basic scenario that was used in ▶ Chap. 2. Remember that a test was given to 40 new hires, and 6 months later, job performance was measured for all of the new hires. Now, let's add one additional piece of information. The group of 40 new hires has two distinct *subgroups*. These subgroups could be based on race, gender, age, disability, etc. For example, the subgroups could be males and females. The exact subgroups for our discussion do not matter at this point. Notice I used the word subgroup. The investigation of test bias using differential prediction involves the analysis of group differences. Specifically, it looks to see if the test *predicts* differently for each subgroup.

Anne Cleary's (1968) approach is probably the most commonly accepted view of differential test prediction and, in fact, of test bias in general. Dr. Cleary was a psychologist and psychometrician who professionally developed high stakes. She had also worked as a university professor, researcher, and administrator. She had a long interest in improving test fairness and understanding group differences. In 1968, she published a highly influential paper. The method she presented would come to be known as the Cleary model of differential prediction. In 1991, she was assigned a student grievance complaint while working at the University of Iowa as Associate Vice President for Academic Affairs. Sadly, the disgruntled student would shoot and kill five individuals, including Anne at the age of 55; leave a sixth individual a quadriplegic (at age 23); and take his own life.

The Cleary approach to bias has been included in professional testing standards and governmental guidelines. Stripped down to the bare bones, her approach states that if your best regression model has more than two lines, then the test exhibits bias. I will not talk about how to decide if one line or two lines are more appropriate, because it is based on statistical modeling and beyond the scope of this book. However, the process can be understood conceptually using graphs. First, a model with a single regression line based on all examines is constructed. Next, a model with two lines, one for each subgroup, is constructed. If the second model with two lines is judged to fit the data better, then there is test bias.

The logic underlying differential test prediction can be illustrated using a series of graphed examples. The examples are enlightening and some of the implications surprising.

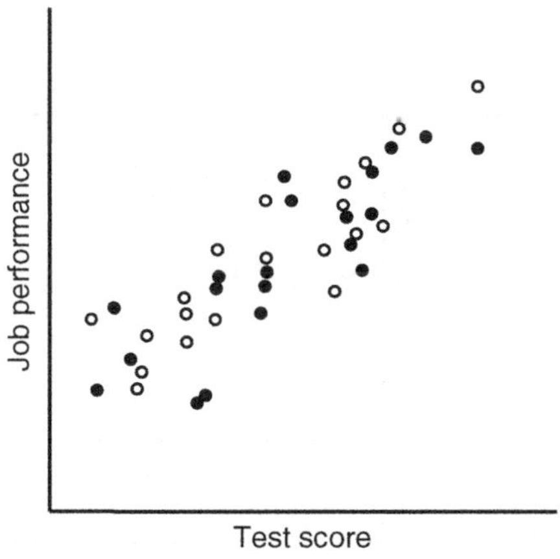

Fig. 3.1 Graph for Example 3.1 showing no test bias

▶ Example 3.1 No Test Bias

Figure 3.1 shows a graph using the same data from ▶ Chap. 2. Only this time I assigned each point to one of two subgroups. Each group is represented by the two colors, and there are 20 white individuals and 20 grey individuals. As you can see, the scores intermix, and to the eye, there appears to be no real difference between groups. We should not, however, simply trust our eyes, because all too often they see what we want them to see.

Let's look at the subgroups individually. (Please note that I will be performing this pseudo analysis backward from what I just stated above concerning the comparison of models, but for this example, I think doing it this way is clearer.) Figure 3.2 shows each subgroup individually with its own regression line fitted to the data.

In Fig. 3.2, the best fitting regression lines look identical. However, with the two side-by-side graphs, it is hard to tell if they really are similar. Therefore, I combine them into a single graph, which is shown in Fig. 3.3. Indeed, the regression lines are the same. They fall right on top of each other. However, to differentiate this from the solid line in Fig. 3.2, I drew it as a dot-dashed line.

According to Cleary's approach, there is no bias in this test. Why? Because test bias involves *differential test prediction*. In this case, there is no difference in the prediction between the two groups. One prediction line fits equally well for both groups. ◀

▶ Example 3.2 No Test Bias with Mean Subgroup Differences

Next, consider the graph shown in Fig. 3.4. In this example, the white subgroup has scored substantially lower than the grey subgroup for both test score and job performance. The difference is easy to see with this small contrived data set, but I drew ellipses around both subgroups to more clearly illustrate this.

As with ▶ Example 3.1, we can plot each group separately and fit a regression line. The slope for each subgroup looks very similar as shown in Fig. 3.5.

Now, we can move on to the next step, combining the two graphs to see if the regression lines are the same. This is shown in Fig. 3.6. The lines fall directly on top each other again (as indicated by the dot-dashed line). Thus, Cleary would say no test bias.

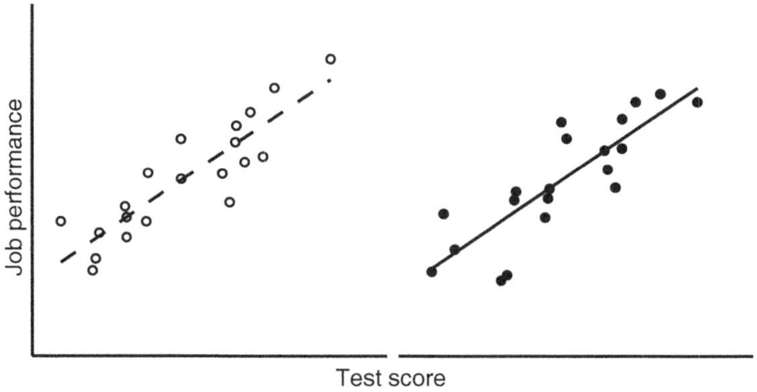

◘ **Fig. 3.2** Graph for Example 3.1 with each subgroup plotted separately with their respective best fitting lines

◘ **Fig. 3.3** Graph for Example 3.1 with a single best fitting regression line

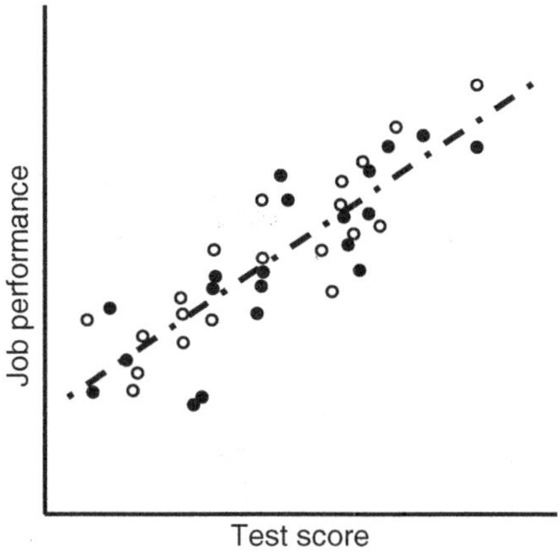

◘ **Fig. 3.4** Graph for Example 3.2 showing no test bias when there are mean subgroup differences

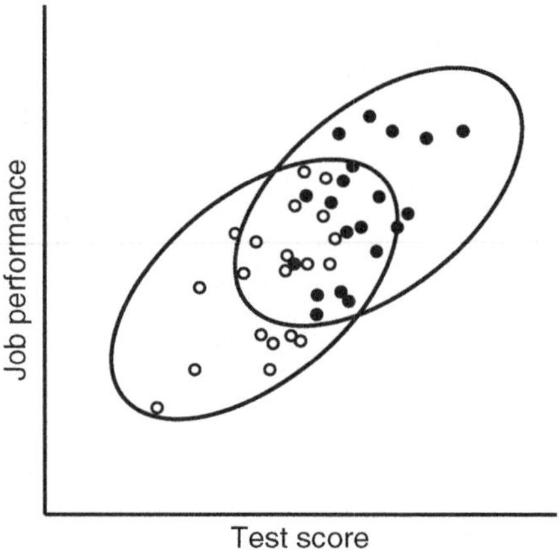

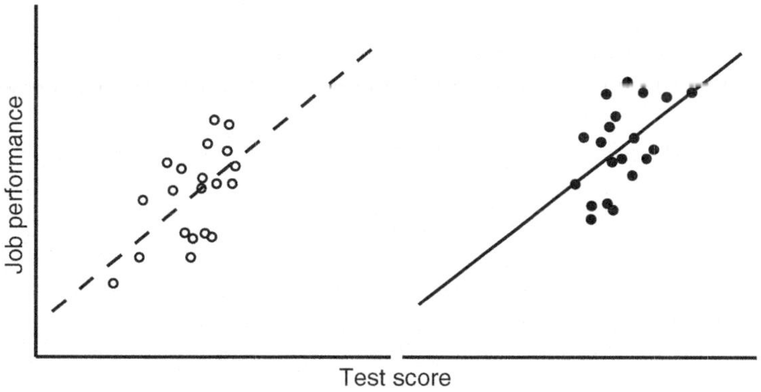

■ **Fig. 3.5** Graph for Example 3.2 with each subgroup plotted separately with their respective best fitting lines

■ **Fig. 3.6** Graph for Example 3.2 with a single best fitting regression line

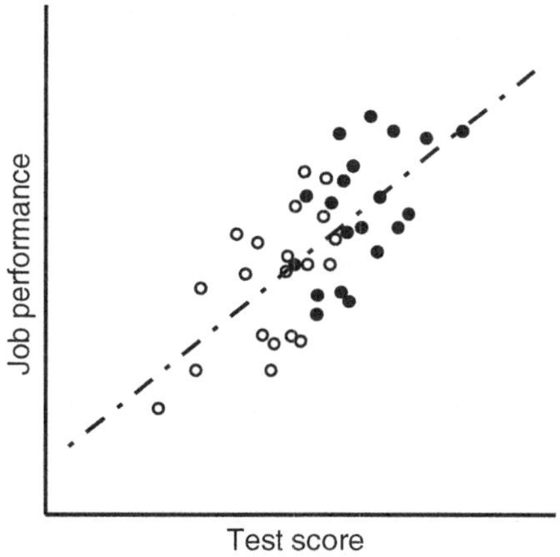

Why? Because one line fits the scores as well as the two separate lines. The test predicts exactly the same for each group. And, the test has the same accuracy for each group.

You may think that this does not make any sense. Obviously, the white subgroup scored less than the grey subgroup on the test. This is where test bias begins to get tricky. Yes, there was a *mean subgroup difference* for the test score. The test, however, predicted equally well for each subgroup. Test validity is based on the accuracy of prediction, not on what any subgroup scores. It just so happened that one subgroup scored lower than the other. In terms of prediction, the test predicted accurately for each group. The fact that one group scored lower is not proof of bias. There could actually be true subgroup differences.

Consider lactose intolerance among ethnic/racial groups. It is well-known that some racial groups tend to be more lactose intolerant than other groups. Is the test biased? Of course not. The test is accurately portraying the difference between the groups. Next, we will see that there can be test bias when in fact there is actually no group differences in test score. The next few of examples will clear a lot of this up, so please stick with me. Test bias only appears simple. This perhaps is one of the reasons so few really understand it. With a little patience, you will be one of the few who do. ◄

3

► Example 3.3 Test Bias with No Mean Difference in Test Score

We will now get into some interesting examples. The last example showed that one group can score lower on a test and the test still be valid with no test bias. Now, consider ◘ Fig. 3.7.

Notice that the white and grey subgroups have roughly the same range of test scores. In addition, it looks like they have the same mean test score. However, for job performance, it appears that there is a tendency for the white group to score lower and the grey group to score higher. To make this clearer, ◘ Fig. 3.8 draws dotted lines for the mean test score for each subgroup and the mean job performance for each subgroup. When a set of scores has these characteristics, the result is test bias. This comes as a surprise to many readers. Most people would see that both subgroups have the same average test score and never even consider that there could be test bias. The rest of this section will explain why there is bias under these circumstances.

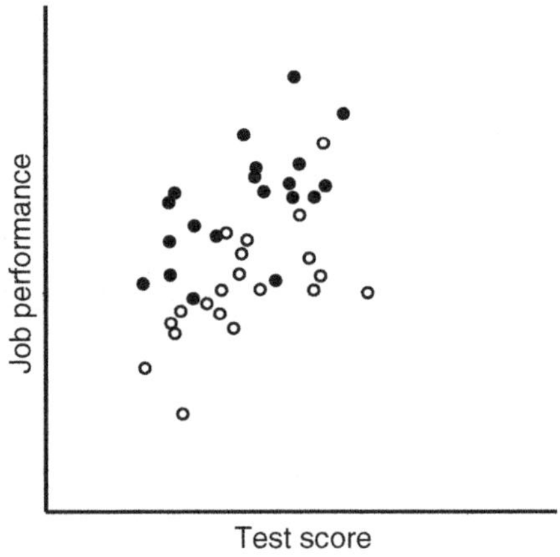

◘ **Fig. 3.7** Graph for Example 3.7 showing test bias with no mean difference in test score

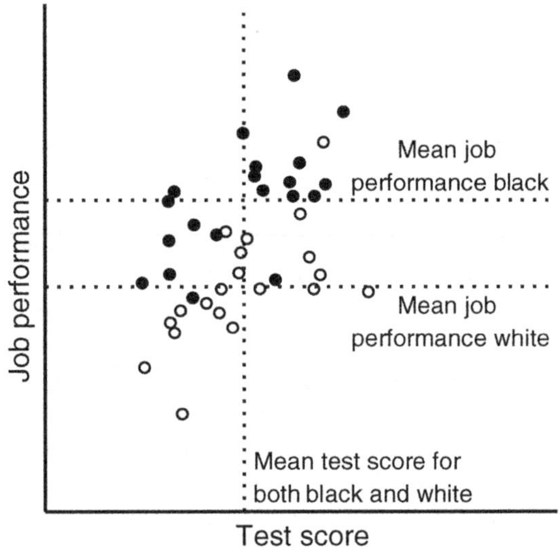

◘ **Fig. 3.8** Graph for Example 3.3 showing mean test score and mean job performance for each subgroup

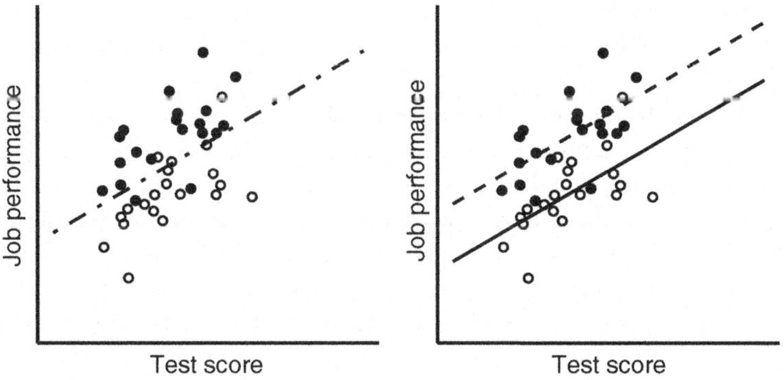

Fig. 3.9 Graph for Example 3.3 showing a single best fitting regression line and separate regression lines for each subgroup

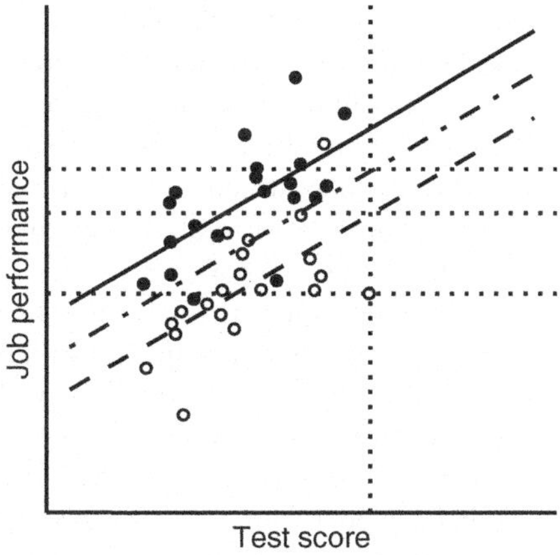

Fig. 3.10 Graph for Example 3.3 showing all three regression lines and mean test score and mean job performance in a single plot

Recall that differential test prediction involves fitting several regression lines to the test scores. Figure 3.9 has two graphs. The graph on the left shows a single regression line fitted to all of the data points. The graph on the right fits a regression line for each subgroup separately. In this case, without any fancy statistics and just eyeballing it, you can see two lines fit the data better than one. Because the grey scores tend to be higher than the white scores, the solid line fits the grey points quite well. The same is true for the dashed line, which fits the white points well. It is lower and, thereby, closer to the white points. When compared to the graph on the left with a single regression line, we can see that the overall regression line in the left-side graph does not fit either group well. It is too low for the grey subgroup and too high for the white subgroup. If we calculated the distance of each point from the regression line, we would find that the amount of prediction error is less when we use two lines in comparison to when we use one line.

Figure 3.10 clarifies our current situation a bit more. In this figure, all three regression lines are in the graph. In a real testing situation, we would most likely hire people who have a high-test score, so I will choose a high scoring white individual to examine more closely. For this white individual, I draw a vertical dotted line up through the point and to each regression line. To predict this individual's job performance, I draw dotted horizontal lines. The bottom horizontal line indicates this person's actual job performance. The middle horizontal dotted line indicates what we would predict the person's job performance to be if we fitted regression lines separately for white and grey individuals. Finally, the top horizontal dotted line indicates what we would predict job performance to be if we fitted a regression line, ignoring a subgroup membership using the single overall regression line.

Examination of these horizontal dotted lines illustrates several findings. First, regardless of the line that is used, there is an inaccuracy in the prediction. Given the variability in people, it is impossible to have a perfect prediction. Our goal is to reduce this error as much as possible. Second, using the model that has two regression lines fitted separately, there is an overprediction in job performance for this individual. Third, if the single regression line model is used, then there is an overprediction in job performance, and this is greater than if we used the dashed regression line for the white subgroup. This leads to the following conclusion: because our goal is to be as accurate as possible, we should use the model with two regression lines, one for white and one for grey. This will result in the least amount of prediction error in job performance. If we calculate the total amount of error for white when we used the dashed line and the total amount of error for white when we used the single overall regression line (represented by the dot-dashed line), we would find that using the white-specific dashed regression line results in the least amount of total error given our data set. This is a mathematical necessity based on how regression works.

In this example, if you want to be the most accurate in your predictions, you need to use subgroup membership. Test validity is about prediction accuracy, so it seems logical to do this. We could do the same with the grey scores. For example, if you wanted to predict how a grey individual will perform on the job, we could compare the prediction error using the solid and dot-dashed lines. We would find that we are most accurate using a model with two regression lines. Obviously, we would be better off using the solid line because it *fits* the grey data better, leading to better predictions. Just looking at the graph, we can see that the single overall regression line (dot-dash) falls below most of the grey points while the solid regression line runs through the middle of the grey points. Using the overall regression line (dot-dash), we end up underpredicting the job performance for the grey points.

There is one problem with using the solid line for hiring grey individuals and using the dashed line for hiring white individuals. It is illegal – that is, if the dashed and solid lines are based on different racial groups, sex, national origin, religion, etc. The 1991 Civil Rights Act specifically made this a *prohibited practice*. As a result, we *must* instead use the overall dot-dashed line even though our best statistical model uses both the dashed and solid lines. The implications of having to do this lead to some surprising results, which will be discussed later. ◄

► Example 3.4 Another Example of Test Bias with No Mean Difference in Test Score

In ► Example 3.3, we saw that subgroups can have the same average test score, but there can still be test bias. ► Example 3.4 presents another situation, where there can be test bias when subgroups can have the same mean test score. ◘ Figure 3.11 presents the data.

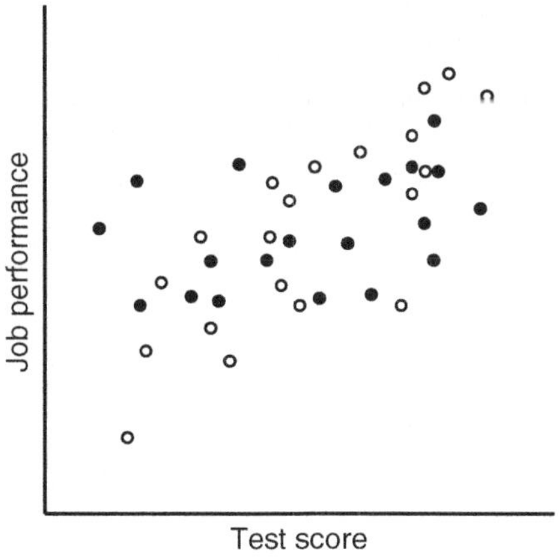

■ **Fig. 3.11** Graph for Example 3.4 showing test bias when there is no difference in mean test score between subgroups

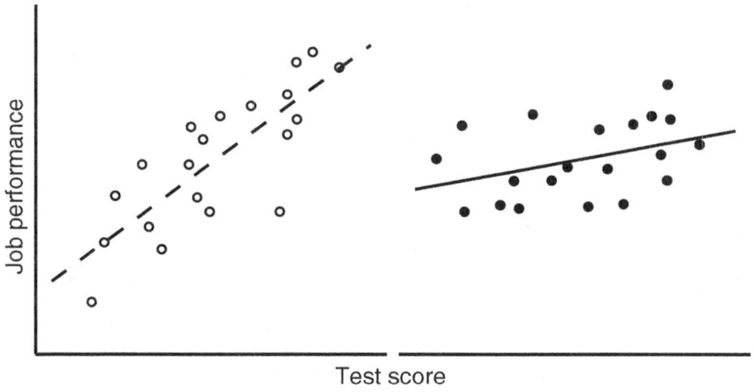

■ **Fig. 3.12** Graph for Example 3.4 with each subgroup plotted separately with their respective best fitting regression line

It is a little hard to clearly see a pattern in ■ Fig. 3.11, so I graph the white and grey subgroups individually and fit a regression line for each subgroup. Looking at the result in ■ Fig. 3.12, we can see that the patterns of the scores for the whites and greys are quite different. For the white points, the line is steeper, while for the grey points, it is flatter. This means that the test has a stronger relationship with job performance for the whites than it does for the greys. If we choose a white individual, we can be more confident that a high-test score will result in high job performance. With the greys, we would be less sure. Next, we need to examine what happens if we graph a single line for all of the individuals ignoring a subgroup membership.

■ Figure 3.13 graphs regression lines for each subgroup individually (solid and dashed lines) and the overall regression line (dot-dashed line) ignoring subgroup membership. In addition, the vertical and horizontal dashed lines show the mean test score and job performance for each subgroup. Each subgroup has the same average test score and job performance. Examination of the three regression lines shows that they are very different from each other. Clearly, when you consider the subgroup membership, the model with the dashed and solid lines fits the data much better than a model that only

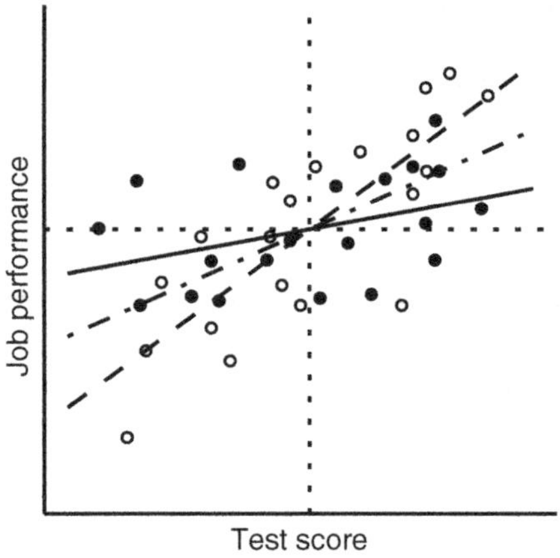

Fig. 3.13 Graph for Example 3.4 showing all three regression lines and mean test score and job performance for each subgroup

has the dot-dashed single overall line. First, notice that the dashed line is steeper than the solid line. In addition, the solid line hits the job performance *y*-axis (job performance) higher than the dashed line does. Finally, the overall dot-dashed line has a still different slope and intercept. In this case, we have different y-intercepts and different slopes. In ► Example 3.3, the lines only differed in where they touched the y-axis. They had the same slopes.

Next, we explore some of the implications of a data that looks like Fig. 3.13. Interestingly, in this situation, each subgroup has the same mean test score shown by the vertical dotted line. Hence, there is no mean difference in the test scores between the white and grey subgroups. The horizontal dotted line is the mean job performance for each subgroup, and interestingly there no difference in the average job performance. However, the Cleary method of differential test prediction indicates that there is test bias in this example.

To understand why there is differential prediction, consider a high scoring white individual. Our best prediction model that minimizes overall error is to use two regression lines. One for the white subgroup and one for the grey subgroup. However, we cannot use two lines, and we must use the single overall regression line (dot-dashed) based on all of the data, ignoring group membership. We are most likely interested in high scoring individuals, so we will examine all points above the mean test score. First, we consider the white points. If we use the dot-dashed line rather than the dashed line, we tend to underpredict their job performance more than if we use the dashed line. Next, let's consider the grey points above the mean. If we use the dot-dashed line rather than the solid line, we tend to overpredict their performance more than if we use the better fitting solid line.

Now, if we only examine the scores less than the mean test score, then the situation is reversed. For the whites, we would overpredict job performance more with the dot-dashed line than if we used the dashed line. For the greys, we would underpredict job performance more using the dot-dashed line than if we used the solid line.

All of this can be summarized as follows. First, the test has differential prediction because two regression lines, one for each subgroup, fit the data better than a single overall regression line. Thus, it predicts differently for the white and grey subgroups.

Second, if we only consider the scores above the mean and use the single regression line model, the test predictions tend to hurt the whites and help the greys. Third, if we only consider scores below the mean and use the overall regression line, the test predictions tend to help the whites and hurt the greys. Fourth, if the subgroups are based on any legally protected class status, such as race, we must use the single regression line. As a result, we introduce more measurement errors using the grey regression line than if we used better fitting model with regression lines for each subgroup. ◀

3.1 Further Explanation of ▶ Examples 3.3 and 3.4

Earlier in ▶ Chap. 2, the formula for a line presented the following:

$$Y' = bX + a$$

- Y' is the value we are trying to predict (the criterion value in this case job performance).
- b is the slope of the line.
- X is the value of x that we are using to predict Y' (is the test score).
- a is the point that the line crosses the y-axis (in this case the job performance axis).

We can apply the concepts we learned in ▶ Examples 3.3 and 3.4 to this equation. In ▶ Example 3.3, the slopes of the dashed (white) and solid (grey) line are the same. This is known because the lines are parallel to each other. As a result, each line has the same value for b. However, the two lines intercept the y-axis at different places. Thus, they have different values for a.

In ▶ Example 3.4, the slopes of the dashed (white) and solid (grey) lines are different, which means the regression lines have different values for b. In addition, they have different y-intercepts, so they have different values for a.

Putting this all together, we can see that anytime we fit two separate regression lines for subgroups and the slope or intercept values are different, there is test bias. This makes sense, because if the slope and intercept values were the same, then the lines would fall right on top of each other, and the test would predict exactly the same for each subgroup.

In reality, it is nearly impossible to have two identical regression lines for subgroups. That is where statistical testing comes into play. At the beginning of this chapter, the logic of the differential test prediction was stated as evaluating two statistical models. The first model has a single regression line applied to both subgroups. The second model has a regression line fitted individual to each subgroup. Statistical methods are then applied to determine if the second model fits the data significantly better than the first model. If it does, then the test predicts differently for each subgroup. We know that the slope and/or y-intercepts for the lines must be different.

One the other hand, if the statistical tests indicate that the models are basically the same, then we know there is no differential prediction. When two lines are fitted, the slope and y-intercepts are essentially the same, and one overall regression line works just fine. The test predicts the same for each subgroup.

▶ Example 3.5 Test Bias with Unequal Group Size

Up to this point, we have looked at simple contrived examples with the subgroups containing equal numbers of individuals. However, this is highly unlikely in practice. In ▶ Example 3.5, the number of individuals in each subgroup will be different. Here is the scenario. We give a test to 80 newly hired people on their first day on the job. We record their scores, wait 6 months, and assess their job performance. One group has 66 individuals, and the other group has 14 individuals. ◘ Figure 3.14 graphs this data.

Although the graph is crowded with more points, careful inspection shows several characteristics of the data. First, the white subgroup has a lot more dots. This will have an important implication later. Second, the two subgroups have the same general pattern of scores. They go from lower left to upper right, indicating that as test score improves, so does job performance. Thus, the test is a valid predictor and can be successfully used to select individuals, and organizations will benefit by using it. Third, the regression lines fitted to each subgroup will be approximately parallel; in other words, they have the same slope. Fourth, regression lines fitted to both groups will have different job performance or y-intercepts. Fifth, it looks like the grey group has a lower average test score and lower job performance. To make these tentative conclusions more apparent, ◘ Fig. 3.15 graphs each group separately with their own regression line and draws dotted lines for the mean test score and job performance for each group. This graph essentially confirms the observations.

Next, we must decide if the single overall regression line fits the data better than two regression lines. ◘ Figure 3.16 shows a graph with all three regression lines fitted to the data. Notice that the dot-dashed overall regression line is not parallel to the separately fitted regression lines. Thus, it has a different slope. This is the result of the unequal subgroup sizes. The overall regression line has a different slope, because the grey dots are not evenly spread out over the entire range of scores. Essentially, the grey dots pull down the overall regression line on the left side of the graph. In addition, because there

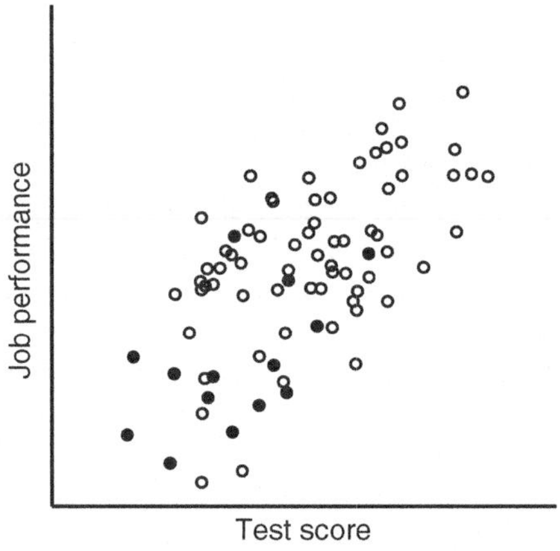

◘ **Fig. 3.14** Graph for Example 3.5 showing test bias with subgroups of different sizes

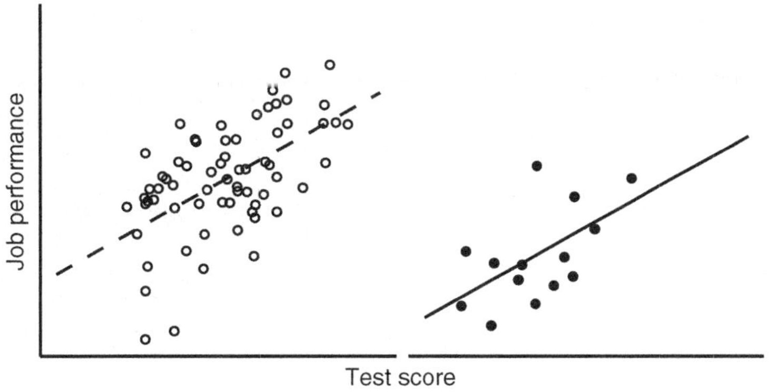

Fig. 3.15 Graph for Example 3.5 showing each subgroup plotted individually with their respective best fitting line

Fig. 3.16 Graph for Example 3.5 showing all three regression lines

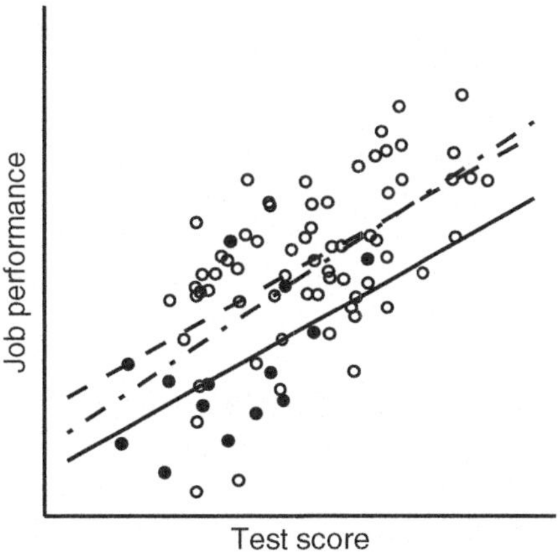

are fewer greys on the right side of the graph, the whites are weighted more heavily, and the overall regression line raises in that area.

► Examples 3.3 and 3.4 showed how over- and underprediction can occur when the overall regression line is used rather than the two separate regression lines. Over- and underprediction occur in this example as well, and the amount of error in prediction varies, depending on the test score and the group. Remember that the amount of error in the prediction is the distance between the separate regression lines and the overall regression line.

Assume that we gave the test to two new people applying for the job and they both fall into the grey subgroup, which is a protected class (it could be gender, race, etc.). One person achieves the highest test score, and this is represented by the up-triangle in Fig. 3.17. The other person obtains the lowest score in the test, and this is represented by the down-triangle. Wanting to be as accurate as possibly, we would like to use the solid line to predict each individual's job performance. However, because subgroup membership is based on a protected class status, we must use the overall dot-dashed regression line according to the 1991 CRA. The distance between the solid and dot-dashed lines is the amount extra error in prediction because of this requirement. For

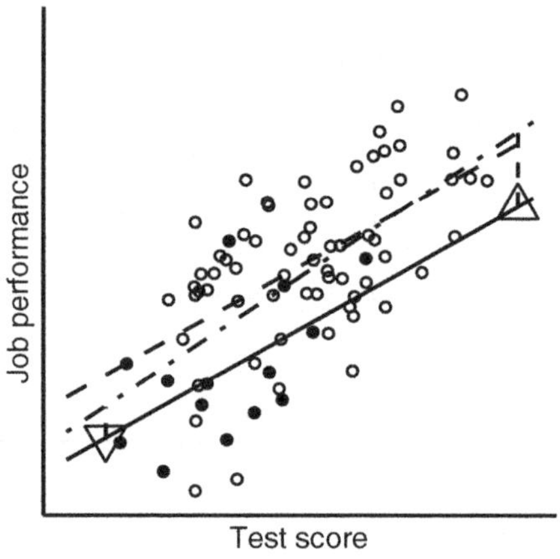

Fig. 3.17 Graph for Example 3.5 showing the prediction implications when there is test bias with unequal subgroup sizes

3

the low scoring new applicant, there is a small amount of overprediction of job performance. However, the overprediction of job performance is much greater for the high scoring new applicant. This overprediction is represented by the dashed lines. To make matters worse, we are most likely to only hire high scoring applicants, which is the area where there is the greatest amount of overprediction. If we consider the white subgroup, for low test scores, job performance is underpredicted, but for high-test scores, job performance is slightly overpredicted. ◄

3.2 Further Explanation of ► Example 3.5

► Example 3.5 is more realistic than the previous examples. The majority group generally has a lot more people in it and generally higher scores. Thus, the overall regression line tends to be closer to the regression line for the majority group when lines are fitted separately.

However, majority performance tends to be underpredicted. In contrast, when the overall regression line is used to predict scores, not only is there an increased error in the prediction of job performance, but also it is in the direction of overprediction. This overprediction actually rewards minority candidates.

In an ironic way, the 1991 CRA act results in an increased measurement error over what we would have if we used our best statistical model. Some might say that is test bias, and there is merit to that idea. An important distinction must be made between bias and fairness. Bias is a technical term that refers to validity and measurement error. Fairness, when used by testing experts, also has a technical meaning that refers to an equitable treatment of all examines. However, the way it is used elsewhere, fairness is more a social construct that is open to a broad range of interpretations based on philosophical, political, etc. ideals.

This is a pretty simple example, but the basic issues closely match what often happens with real testing situations. It also illustrates how things can quickly become complicated. With testing being a highly emotional issue and so many people not being well versed in the topic, fairly simple measurement concepts like this are rarely discussed or understood.

A lot of testing "issues" are not really testing issues. They are societal, legal, political, resource, etc. issues. How much should the measurement expert get involved in these issues? And conversely, how much should the social agenda, politics, etc. influence the measurement issues? That is an open question.

The effect shown above has been demonstrated many times in the measurement literature. When tests show differences in mean test scores for subgroups, the tests themselves are attacked as the source of the problem. However, it is often overlooked that there are corresponding differences on things, such as graduation rates, access to materials, etc. The tests are easy targets, because they are something that most have some general dislike for anyway. Think about the alternative explanation though – the tests are in fact bias. This would mean that the tests are creating group differences rather than accurately reporting them. If this is the case, then there is little to no need for society to work to correct any social inequalities. The differences are only an artifact of the test. Programs, like Head Start, are not important, because after all it is the test that is causing the problems. Granted, I am taking this to the extreme, but there is merit to this logic.

The alternative explanation is that the test is accurately reflecting subgroup differences on both the predictor (the test) and the outcome (the criterion, in this case job performance). Those who are not involved in measurement often forget the criterion. If the test is measuring factors that are important on the job, then it makes sense that there would be a corresponding deficit on the criterion (job performance) as well. We always need to keep in mind that we must not only measure the predictor accurately but also the criterion as well. This is often forgotten.

In the measurement world, it is commonly known that creating better tests will not reduce these differences, if subgroup differences actually exist. In fact, better, more reliable, and valid tests will actually exacerbate the problem and highlight the difference even more. In addition, a common criticism of tests is that they are flawed, because they do not measure all determinants of success. Any test can be criticized for what it does not measure. For example, a thermometer only measures air temperature. It does not measure humidity, wind speed, etc., which are all important if someone is going to experience heat exhaustion or hypothermia. Do we say the thermometer is biased? No, it measures something that is very important to determining heat exhaustion, but it cannot tell you everything. It would be nice if we had unlimited resources and could test without regard to our limited resources. We cannot. As a result, we employ tests that are incomplete measures, but they are still highly useful. In fact, standardized tests consistently have been found to be better than the other unstandardized alternatives that can be more easily manipulated and potentially have more bias.

If the differences are cause by social inequities, poverty, poor prenatal care, nutrition, and so on, the differences will only disappear when these factors are eliminated. The classes or groups that are used in analyses, such as differential prediction, are just an easily identifiable factor, and the test is just the messenger. Measurement experts think about these things all the time and work hard to have the most accurate measurement possible. For some reason though, they get put in an unwinnable situation — create psychometrically sound tests, with limited resources, and achieve competing and, at times, conflicting social, economic, and political ideals.

3.3 Summary

Differential prediction is the most widely understood and widely used approach to test bias. In addition, it has a long history of use and a substantial body of research supporting it. In this chapter, we found that the commonly accepted view of different average test scores between groups is, in fact, *not* bias. Instead, test bias from a psychometric differential prediction point of view is a result of a poorly fitting overall regression line. If fitting regression lines individually to subgroups substantially improves our accuracy, then there is test bias. The test predicts differently for each subgroup.

To complicate the matter, the 1991 CRA requires that a single overall regression line be used when predicting. This causes increased measurement error beyond what we would have if we used the best fitting model. This can create systematic over- and underprediction for the subgroups and lead to unexpected results.

Discussion Questions

1. According to differential prediction, differences in the average subgroup performance do not necessarily result in test bias. Why is this? Include illustrative graphs in your explanation.
2. Explain how there can be differential prediction or test bias even if both subgroups have the same average test score. Include illustrative graphs in your explanation.
3. The differential prediction approach uses linear regression to detect test bias. Provide examples of the different ways in which test bias occurs based on the slope and y-intercept of regression lines.
4. Why does the single overall regression line generally result in a more accurate prediction for the majority group in comparison to the minority group?
5. Construct a graph showing how a test can at times overpredict performance for a minority group and at times underpredict performance for a minority group and provide a written explanation.

References

Civil Rights Act of 1991 § 109, 42 U.S.C. § 2000e et seq (1991).

Cleary, T. A. (1968). Test bias: Prediction of grades of Negro and White students in integrated colleges. *Journal of Educational Measurement, 5*, 115–124.

Measurement Variance

Contents

T. A. Stetz, *Test Bias in Employment Selection Testing*, Classroom Companion: Business, https://doi.org/10.1007/978-3-030-89925-7_4

Objectives

- Explain what are psychological construct and why it is hard to measure them.
- Explain why measurement variance (or measurement invariance) is called an internal approach to test bias.
- Describe the basic logic behind the measurement variance approach to bias.
- Provide an example of how measurement variance is used in testing.
- Explain how confirmatory factor analysis can be used to assess construct validity and measurement variance.

The last chapter covered differential prediction, as in the Cleary model of test bias. However, there are other ways to think about test bias, and these ways are more technical and complicated. While the underlying mathematics and statistics are complicated, the concepts behind the approaches are easily understood. Therefore, once again I will strip away the mathematical complexities and use graphs to demonstrate the ideas behind the approach.

This chapter will cover *measurement variance* or *measurement inequivalence*. Variance is very important in measurement. That is because for measurements to be useful, the numbers must vary. If everyone was the same, there would be no point to measurement. Measure one person and you know everything about all the people. Imagine Image the graphs from the last chapter. If everyone was the same, then every graph would have one dot with all the examinees piled on top of each other. Anyone could (or could not) do a job. Everyone would have the same exact test score and job performance. Everyone would have the same level of psychological adjustment. Everyone would have the same sense of humor, which would be good unless it was a bad humor. While I long for sameness, as it would make everything so much easier, it is unrealistic. For tests to be useful, people must vary. Furthermore, if tests and measurements are to be valid, the items must vary in specific ways. And, they must vary similarly across subgroups. In this chapter, we will examine bias as a function of the relationships among the test items.

4.1 Psychological Constructs and Measurement Invariance

Psychological measurement is concerned with *constructs*. A construct is theoretical. It is abstract. It is an underlying trait, characteristic, or aspect of a person. A psychological construct cannot be directly observed like height or hair color. Instead, they must be inferred by measurements that we perform. Using various methods, we can assign a number describing a person's level of accounting knowledge or assign a number to indicate his or her level of agreeableness. How the items on a test interrelate can provide evidence for the validity of the measurement of the construct.

Suppose you had a test with ten items. Five of the items measured verbal ability and five measured math ability. We would expect the verbal items to be highly related. In other words, if you correctly answered item number 1, we would expect that you could correctly answer item number 2. Thus, your score on item 1 is related to your score on item 2 and so on. In contrast, the correctness of your verbal ability answers should not be *too* related to the correctness of the math questions you answer. We would expect some relationship, but not too much. Items within a construct will likely be highly related to each other, while they will likely be less related to items measuring a different construct. This concept is the key to understanding *construct validity* and *measurement invariance.*

Measurement experts are not just concerned with the total scores. In the development of unbiased tests, it is equally important to examine how each item operates internally within the entire test. We want all our items to operate in the same way for all groups of test takers. It is unrealistic that every item will operate exactly the same, but it is a goal that is strived for. If one subgroup is answering the question in one way and another subgroup in a different way, then this suggests that some irrelevant factor is affecting how the question is being answered.

► Example 4.1 Single Construct Measurement

Suppose we created a four-item English test and administered the test to 20 people. Ten people are from Subgroup 1 and ten are from Subgroup 2. Each question was scored on a 1 to 5 scale with 5 being the highest score. The results of this hypothetical test are shown in ◘ Table 4.1. We can see that each group has the same average score of 13.40. Thus, immediately some would say no bias. In the last chapter, however, we learned that having the same average test score does not ensure that there is no test bias. Also, as discussed above, we need to dig deeper into the internal psychometric properties of the test.

◘ Table 4.1 Example 4.1 data

Group 1					Group 2				
ID	Item 1	Item 2	Item 3	Item 4	ID	Item 1	Item 2	Item 3	Item 4
1	3	4	4	4	11	3	4	4	3
2	4	5	4	4	12	5	5	4	3
3	5	5	4	4	13	5	5	4	4
4	1	2	2	2	14	1	2	3	4
5	2	2	2	3	15	2	2	2	4
6	4	3	4	4	16	3	4	3	2
7	5	4	4	3	17	5	4	5	3
8	5	5	4	4	18	5	5	5	4
9	2	1	3	3	19	2	1	2	3
10	2	2	3	3	20	2	2	3	2

	Subgroup 1	Subgroup 2
Mean score	13.40	13.40

Table 4.2 Example correlation matrix

	Item 1	Item 2	Item 3	Item 4
Item 1				
Item 2	Item 1 and item 2			
Item 3	Item 1 and item 3	Item 2 and item 3		
Item 4	Item 1 and item 4	Item 2 and item 4	Item 3 and item 4	

In the Cleary model, we took the total test score and plotted it against a score on some criterions (in our examples, it was job performance). When we look at the measurement invariance, we will do something quite similar; we will look at the scatterplots of all pairs of items against each other. In other words, we will look at the relationship of item 1 and item 2, item 1 and item 3, etc. Thus, in the Cleary model, we used a criterion that was separate from the test or external to the test. In the measurement variance approach, all of the other items are criterions. Because of this difference, the Cleary model is sometimes called an external approach, and the measurement invariance is called an internal approach to test bias.

With four items, we will have six relationships to examine. These types of relationships are generally shown in a correlation or covariance matrix. A sample matrix is shown in Table 4.2.

Look at the body of the table and locate the cell that has "item 1 and item 2." This means, we will plot the scores of item 1 against the scores of item 2, and then find the best fitting line. The graph will go in that cell. Now look at the cell with "item 3 and item 4." In this cell, we will plot the scores for item 3 and item 4 and find the best fitting line. You may have noticed that there are a lot of empty cells. First, the cells on the diagonal are empty. That is because the relationship between item 1 and item 1 is perfect. It does not give us any useful information. Sometimes, psychometricians do put numbers in the diagonal cells, but we are not going to worry about that. The upper cells are simply mirror images of the lower cells. Thus, go to the second row and third column. This cell would plot item 2 against item 1. This is the same thing as plotting item 1 against item 2 only with the axis switched, so these cells do not carry any new information and are left blank. We could have just as easily used the upper half of the matrix, but the standard practice is to use the lower half of the matrix.

One more thing to remember is that test bias looks at differences across subgroups so we are going to have at least two matrices to compare, one for Subgroup 1 and one for Subgroup 2. We will compare the matrices to see if they look that same. Some of this is going to be a review from concepts of earlier chapters, but it is important to go through this all the way from begging to end.

Figure 4.1 shows the first graph. The horizontal axis is the score for item 1, and the vertical axis is the score for item 2. Remember, left to right and bottom to top are the higher scores. Look at the scores for Subgroup 1. Person 1 had a score of 3 on the first

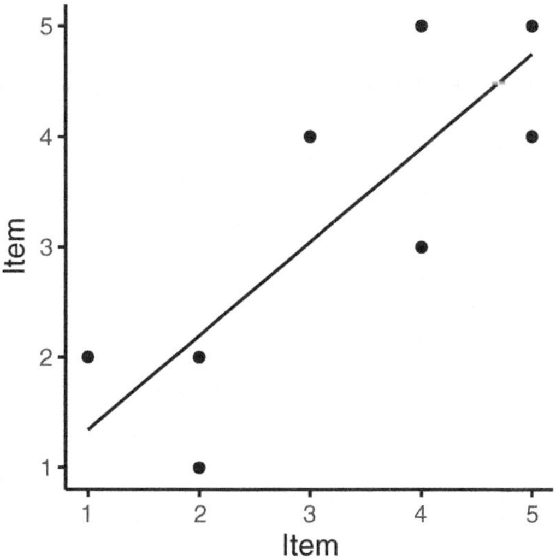

■ **Fig. 4.1** Graph for Example 4.1 showing the relationship between scores on two test items including the regression line

item and a score of 4 on the second. Thus, we go to 3 on the horizontal axis and go up 4 vertically and place a dot there. We then do that for each of the ten people in Subgroup 1. Thus, we will have a scatterplot with ten dots on it. However, counting the points on the graph, there are eight. This is because more than one test taker can have the same scores. In this graph, two people had scores of 5 and 5 and two people had scores of 2 and 2. This can be verified by looking back at ■ Table 4.1.

For these graphs, you would expect a line from the lower left to the upper right corners. If someone gets a higher score on one item, you would expect them to get a higher score on another item (if the items are tapping the same construct). Each item gives a little bit of information about that person's ability. With four items, you have a better idea of that person's standing on the construct than you do with one item. That is why tests can be long. Rarely is a psychological construct measured with a single item. The more questions you ask, the more information you collect and the more you know about that person.

Above, we created a single plot. Now, we need to make five more plots for Subgroup 1 and then repeat the entire process for Subgroup 2. The result of this is shown in ■ Fig. 4.2.

We will walk through this figure row by row. In the top row, compare the graph for Subgroup 1 and Subgroup 2. While the individual dots are in different places, the best fitting lines look nearly identical. This shows that item 1 and item 2 are operating the same way for both groups. It shows that the items covary similarly for both groups. In the second row, there are two graphs. The first graph examines item 1 and item 3, and the second graph examines item 2 and item 3. Once again, the individual points are in somewhat different places, but the best fitting lines look quite similar. This suggests that the items are similarly relating to each other across the subgroups.

Finally, examine the third row. In this row, items 1, 2, and 3 are being graphed with item 4. Looking at this graph, we notice a difference between the two subgroups. First, for Subgroup 1 (the left side of the panel), item 4 is operating as expected. It shows a

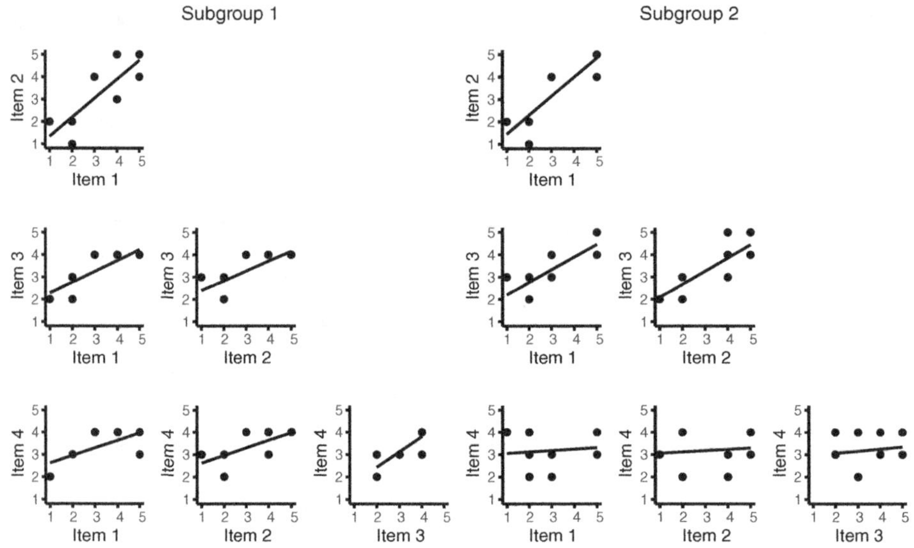

Fig. 4.2 Graphs for Example 4.1 showing interitem correlations for two subgroups

positive relationship with all the items, meaning higher scores on item 4 tend to be associated with higher scores on the other items. Or we could also say the better a Subgroup 1 individual does one any of the first three items, the better they do on item 4. Because all of the items are showing this same general pattern, this provides support for the idea that within Subgroup 1, we are accurately measuring a single underlying construct.

Subgroup 2, however, is different. Look specifically at the last row, which shows the plots involving item 4. First, compare these plots to the other Subgroup 2 plots. We see that the scatterplots and the best fitting lines look very different. For Subgroup 2, there is a much weaker relationship between item 4 and the other items on the test. All the lines are fairly flat, showing that scoring higher on the other items does not necessarily indicate how well a person will score on item 4. Thus, item 4 does not appear to contribute to the accurate measurement of the construct for Subgroup 2.

Now compare the last row across Subgroup 1 and Subgroup 2. Again, we see very different lines. Subgroup 1 has steeper lines than Subgroup 2. All of this suggests that item 4 is working okay for Subgroup 1, but not okay for Subgroup 2. In other words, it is not measuring the same way for both groups, and it leads us to question if we really even know what item 4 is measuring for Subgroup 2. As a result, we cannot interpret the scores for the subgroups the same. If item 4 is measuring something different for Subgroup 2, we should not be adding the scores to come up with a total score. When something like this happens, it is a problem. We say that the test demonstrates *measurement variance* or *measurement inequivalence* across the groups. This is a form of measurement bias.

If all of the graphs looked similar between Subgroup 1 and Subgroup 2, we would say that the test displayed *measurement invariance* or *measurement equivalence*. This piece of evidence gives us greater confidence in the accuracy of our measurement of the given construct.

Of course, this is just a visual depiction of measurement variance. Psychometricians do not use pictures to decide if there was a problem with the test. Instead, they do more complicated analyses. The idea behind the analyses is basically the same as I present here though. The only difference is that they would be using numbers in the body of the matrices. These numbers would probably indicate how the scores on the items *covary*, which is similar to what is shown in the graphs. Then, using a variety of statistical procedures, they would perform statistical tests on those numbers to determine if the patterns of covariation are the same across the groups.

Obviously, measurement invariance is very different from differential prediction. Differential prediction uses the total test score and some outside criterion measure. The relationship between the total test score and the outside criterion can be exactly the same for different subgroups of people. Even though a test may not display bias as defined by differential prediction, this does not guarantee that all items on the test will relate similarly within a test or across subgroups. Thus, we can have no differential prediction at the test level, but we may still have measurement bias in the form of measurement variance within a test. ◄

► Example 4.2 Multiple Constructs in a Single Test

In ► Example 4.2, we will assume we gave a 25-item personality test to 5000 individuals with each item measured on a 1 to 5 scale. Using the same approach describe above would result in a lot of graphs to look at and a lot of scores to put on each graph. In fact, there would be 300 graphs for each group for a total of 600 that would need to be compared. It would be a big uninterruptable blob. Instead of creating each scatterplot and then finding the best fitting line, I am going to use a different visualization technique. I will create a 25 by 25 matrix. The shade of each cell will be based on the strength of the relationship between two items represented by the best fitting line. This sort of visualization is sometimes called a color tile plot or a heat map. ◘ Figure 4.3 shows some examples translating scatterplots and best fitting lines into colors.

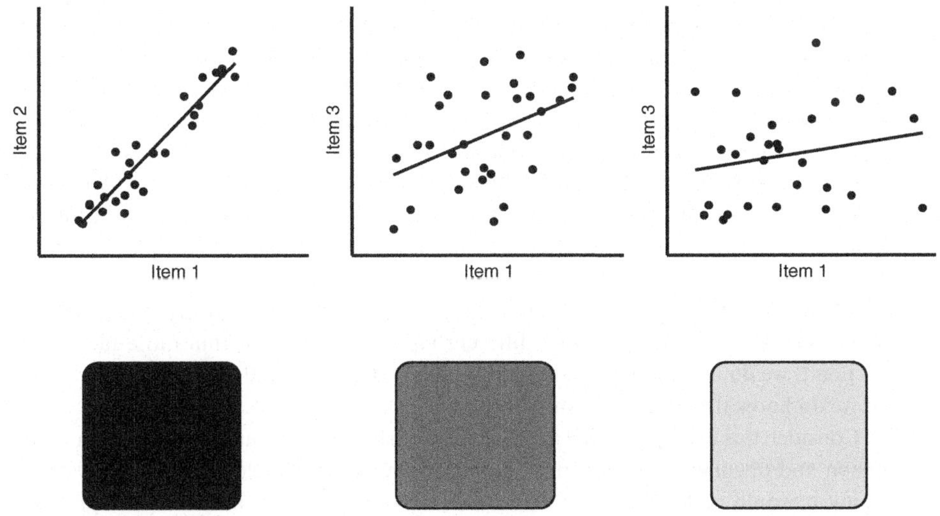

◘ **Fig. 4.3** Graphs translating correlation scatterplots into different colors based on the strength of correlation

The scatterplot for two highly related items might look something like the first graph in ◘ Fig. 4.3. When there is a strong relationship between test items, the cell will be dark grey. Remember, this will represent a strong relationship or tendency for the items to covary together. As the score on one item increases, the score on the other item correspondingly tends to increase. A medium grey cell indicates a weaker relationship with a less steep line and the dots more spread out. This is shown in the second graph in ◘ Fig. 4.3. Finally, a very light grey cell indicates a flat line and dots spread out. A light grey cell shows that there is no (or very) little relationship between the two items.

Looking at these graphs, you can see the shade of the cell is related to how steep the line is and how close the dots are to the line. Dark grey is what you hope to see among items that are supposed to measure the same thing. And light grey is what you hope to see when items are supposed to measure different things. For medium grey, sometimes it is expected, and other times, light grey could be a problem. It just depends on the situation.

Continuing with this example, personality is most commonly thought of as consisting of five different, but related, constructs. The research literature refers to these constructs as factors. The five factors are as follows: emotional stability, extraversion, openness to experience, agreeableness, and conscientiousness. These factors are called the Big Five personality traits, and many people have developed surveys to measure them. You may ask, how do we know that they are different constructs? Measurement variance is the answer.

There have been thousands of Big Five research studies. The example that is presented here is somewhat fictitious but draws on this large body research. Remember in this example we have a 25-item personality test. This test has five items for each Big Five factor. Measurement variance examines how these 25 items interrelate.

◘ Figure 4.4 summarizes the research on the Big Five, showing how the items on our hypothetical Big Five personality test might relate. Notice the triangles of dark grey along the diagonal. Consider the first five questions. We would expect that these items, all measuring emotional stability, would be highly related to each other. The next five items measure extraversion, and we would expect them to all be highly related to each other as well. This continues for each of the Big Five factors. Thus, this pattern of dark grey indicates that within each factor, the items tend to be highly related. This is good because it is evident that the items within each construct are measuring similarly.

If we had found a single large triangle of dark grey cells for the first ten items, that would be a problem. It would suggest that all of these items are highly related. Therefore, rather than measuring two distinct constructs, we are likely measuring a single construct. What this construct is we really do not know, but we would know that emotional stability and Extraversion are not separate factors.

We now know how the items within each factor relate to each other. Next, we need to examine the relationship among different factors and items within those factors. At this point, we do not know if medium grey cells or light grey cells are most appropriate, but we do know that these cells should not be dark grey.

Consider this example. What type of relationship would you expect between extroversion and openness to experience? Based on my informal theories and observations, I think it would make sense that extroverts, in comparison to introverts, are probably more likely to seek out new experiences. We would, therefore, expect a certain degree

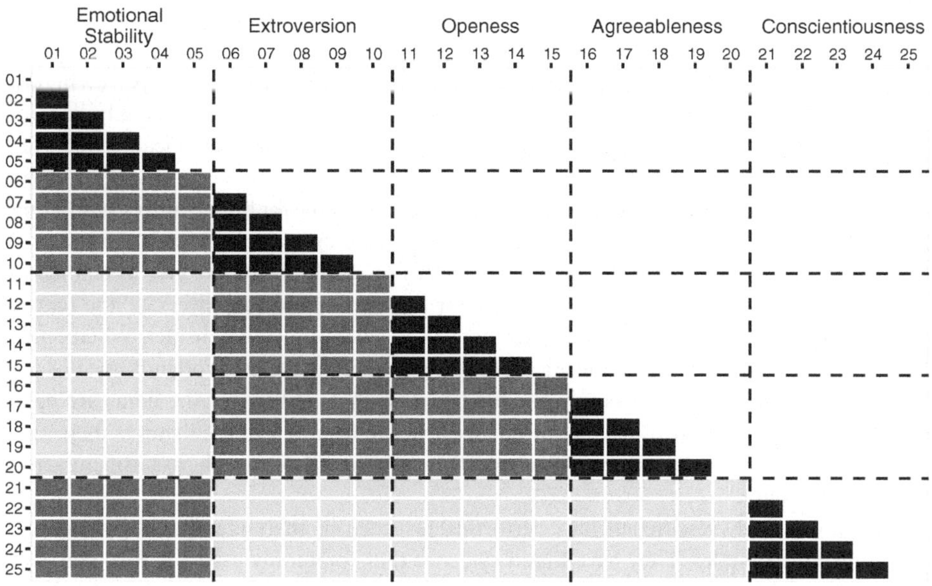

Fig. 4.4 Color tile plot for Example 4.2 showing construct variance commonly found for Big Five personality assessments

of relationship between the two measures. Of course, the items within the extroversion scale should be more highly related to each other than they would be to the items on the openness scale. This is exactly what we see. Within each factor, the items are highly related as indicated by the dark grey cells. Now read across rows 11–15 (openness) and down columns 6–10 (extroversion) to where they intersect. The cells are medium grey, indicating a moderate degree of relationship, not as strong as within each factor, but not totally unrelated either. Thus, this confirms our informal hypotheses and supports the construct validity of our hypothetical measurement device.

Consider another example. Look across rows 21–25 that correspond to conscientiousness. I cannot think of a good reason why this factor would be strongly or moderately related to most of the other factors. Notice that most of these cells are light grey, indicating little to no relationship with the other factors. The one exception is columns 1–5, which correspond to emotional stability. Now that I think of it, my informal observations would support this too, so this pattern of relationships seems to make sense. Most emotionally unstable people are probably not very conscientious. Thus, we have (informally) established some degree of construct validity for our hypothetical Big Five personality measure.

With a better understating of measurement variance and construct validity, we can apply this newly found knowledge to test bias in the form of measurement variance. ◄

► Example 4.3 Measurement Variance and Cross-Cultural Personality Measurement

Suppose a company has been using our 25-item big-five personality assessment for several years to hire employees in the USA. This company would now like to use the same measure to hire employees in India. Everyone who will be hired speaks English, so translation and language issues are at a minimum. Even though the test has been successfully used in the USA and shows no construct-related measurement problems, there are substantial cultural differences between the USA and India. Therefore, it is possible that the big-five scale may not display the same internal psychometric properties in both countries. It needs to be shown that there is construct equivalence across the Indian and US employees. For if there is no equivalence, the measurements could lead to incorrect conclusions.

To determine that the assessment is measuring the same for both countries, we would need to give the assessment to a group of Indian employees and compare the results to US employees. No difference among the pattern of relationships will give us confidence that the assessment is working the same for both groups of employees. If the pattern of relationships is not the same, then there are a few options to consider. When only a small number of items are causing problems, you can remove these offending items and rerun the analysis. The reason you would remove them is because the items are being interpreted differently by each group. Thus, it would be unfair to use them. If there are a lot of items that are operating differently, then you should not use the assessment across the two groups.

Interestingly, researchers have performed just such an analysis across many countries using large samples. They have found evidence that commonly used Big Five personality assessments display construct equivalence across the US and Indian samples. Thus, ◘ Fig. 4.5 illustrates what this would look like using our visualization from ◘ Fig. 4.4. We cannot just assume that because others have shown construct equivalence, it is okay to use our particular Big Five assessment. There is a saying that all validation is local. Basically, this means that you should check for yourself that our Big Five assessment is consistent across our groups. I should note that many measurement experts are pro-

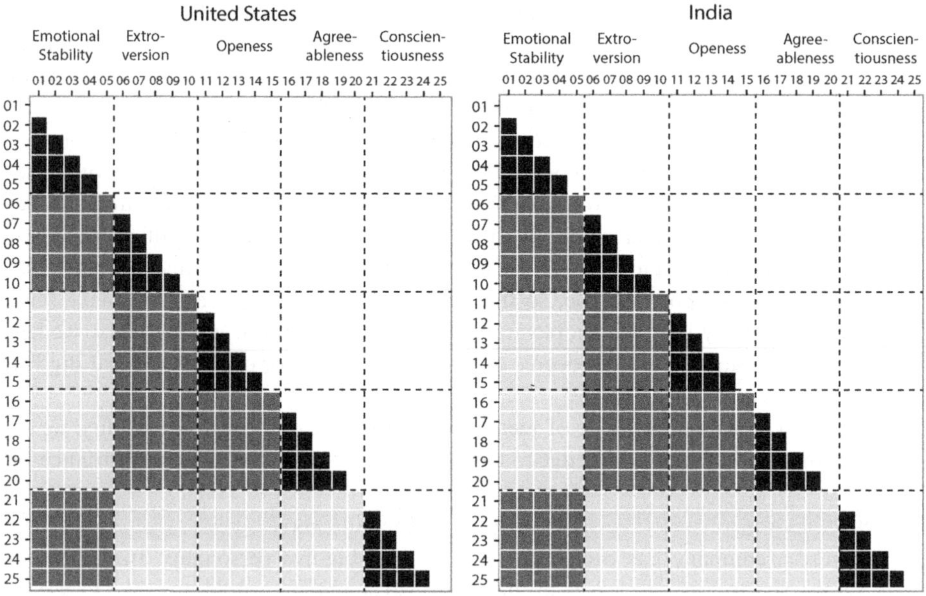

◘ **Fig. 4.5** Color tile plot showing construct equivalence between the United States and India on a hypothetical Big Five personality assessment

ponents of *validity generalization*. This view of validity asserts that if there is strong validity evidence for a test, you should be able to safely use the test in other situations similar to where the validity has already been demonstrated. There is scientific evidence to support this, but testing is also about a lot of other things than science. The safest option is to perform your own validity study even though it might not strictly be needed based on scientific evidence.

Figure 4.6 shows what it might look like if there is measurement variance across the US and Indian employees. In this graph, it can be seen that there are differences in how the items are operating. The relationships among the items vary between the two groups, suggesting that the US and Indian employees interpret the items differently. In particular, items 20 and 25 appear to be operating differently between the two countries. Because of this, the scores do not mean the same thing for each group, and the assessment should not be used as it currently exists. One possible solution, rather than creating an entirely new assessment, would be to simply drop the items that are causing the problems. Thus, items 20 and 25 could be removed, and the assessment could be used with the 23 remaining items.

Realize, however, that even if there is construct equivalence, indicated by the pattern of relationships among the items, it does not mean that the US and Indian employees will have the same level of extroversion, openness, etc. There are real cultural differences between these countries. In ▶ Chap. 3, it was stated that a mean difference between subgroups does not indicate bias. For example, East Asian countries score lower on openness to experience than Latin American countries. This is not biased by the measurement instrument. Rather, the measurement instrument is accurately reflecting those two cultures.

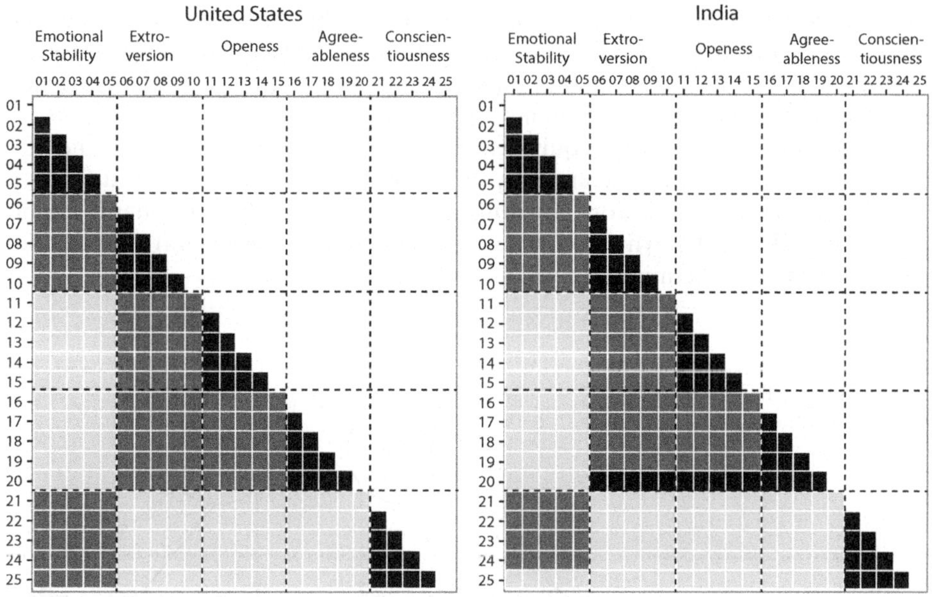

Fig. 4.6 Color tile plot showing construct inequivalence between the United States and India on a hypothetical Big Five construct assessment

Equivalence or invariance looks at the relationships of items to ensure that they are operating the same across subgroups. If the patterns are the same across subgroups, this is an important piece of information, suggesting that measurement bias is not a problem. However, if there are inconsistencies in how the item relate among themselves, then this suggests a problem that should be further investigated. ◄

4.2 Confirmatory Factor Analysis

In ► Chaps. 2 and 3, the mathematical ideas behind the test bias approach were presented first, and then examples demonstrating them were presented. Here, however, I believe presenting first the examples and then discussing the statistical approach work better. Psychometricians and test developers use a statistical technique called confirmatory factor analysis, or CFA, to determine if there is measurement equivalence across groups. CFA allows us to determine how well a hypothesized measurement model fits the observed or collected data and then allows us to determine if the model is the same for different groups. CFA is a specific application of a technique called structural equation modeling (SEM). This approach typically uses diagrams as shown in ◘ Fig. 4.7.

◘ Figure 4.7 depicts a six-item test that measures verbal and math ability. Three items measure verbal ability and three items measure math ability. In CFA, the rectangles represent measured or *observed* variables. These are actually test questions. Since we have the scores for everyone taking the test, we call these observed. Circles represent our constructs. These are *unobserved* because we can only infer that they exist based on our observed or measured items. As a result, unobserved constructs are called *latent variables* in CFA. The arrows, however, point from the latent construct to the observed variables. This is because the construct is a characteristic of a person and, as a result, influences how they answer the questions. For example, a person's knowledge of accounting (a latent construct) will determine how they answer items on an accounting test.

Demonstrating construct equivalence can be a detailed procedure, and this explanation is very limited. Generally, the underlying structure of the variables is first demonstrated. This is done by fitting a model that only has one latent variable as shown in ◘ Fig. 4.8, which proposes that there is only one general ability factor that is driving how examinees score on the six items.

◘ **Fig. 4.7** Confirmatory Factor Analysis diagram with two distinct constructs

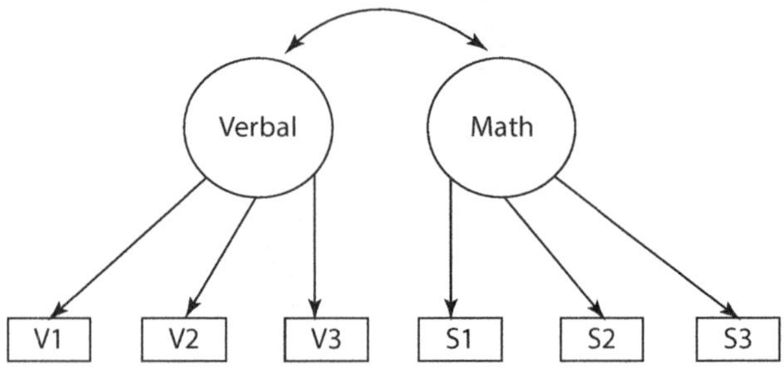

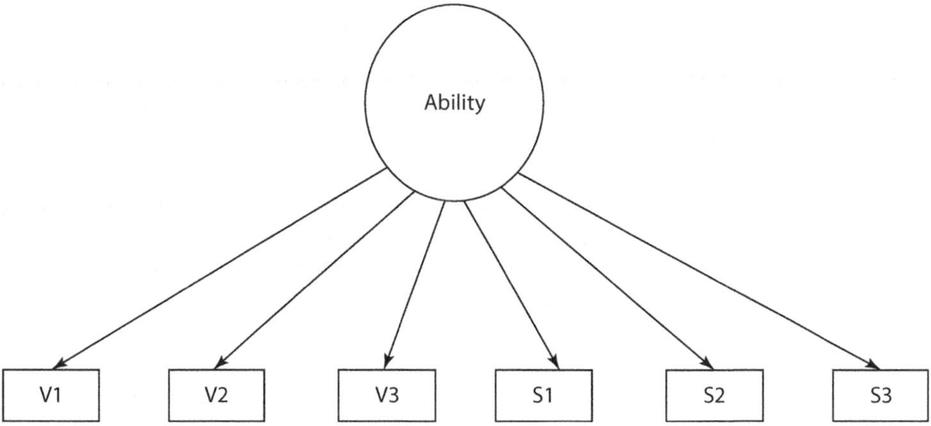

Fig. 4.8 Confirmatory Factor Analysis diagram with a single construct

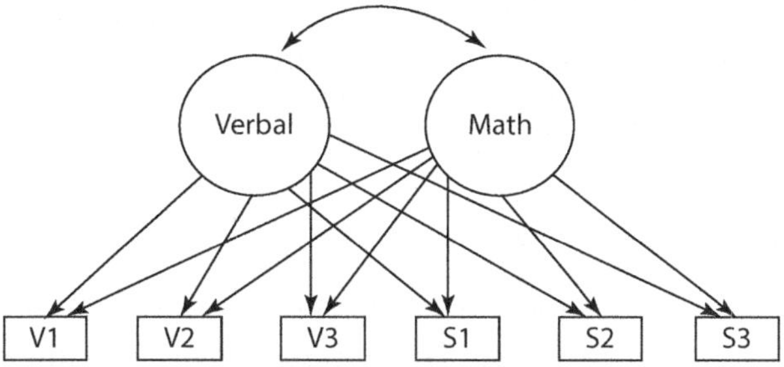

Fig. 4.9 Confirmatory Factor Analysis diagram showing two related constructs

Next, the model with two latent variables is fitted like the one in Fig. 4.9. In this model, both latent factors influence how examinees answer the questions. However, remember our earlier matrix figure with the big-five assessment. Items within a construct are highly related, in which CFA is similar to saying they *load* heavily on the same latent variable, and this was represented by the shade of grey. Thus, conceptually the arrows between the verbal latent construct and items V1, V2, and V3 would be dark grey. The arrows between the math latent construct and items V1, V2, and V3 would be medium or light grey. Thus, items from one construct should load heavily on their own construct and not too heavily on a different construct.

The process of establishing measurement invariance might start with Fig. 4.8 that has a single latent variable. We would use this as a baseline to compare later models. Next, we might fit the model shown in Fig. 4.9 and compare it to the first model. If it does not fit significantly worse, we could move on to the model shown in Fig. 4.7. In Fig. 4.7, we do not expect the verbal items to load on the math construct nor do we expect the math items to load on the verbal construct. If this model fits as well as the previous two, then this would provide evidence, supporting the idea that the test is measuring two distinct constructs, and given our knowledge of the test questions, we assume it is verbal ability and math ability. It is important to understand that this does not prove that our model is absolutely correct. However, if it makes theoretical sense, in this case verbal and math ability being separate constructs does, then our analysis adds confidence to our belief in what the test is measuring.

Now that we have established a level of confidence that our test is measuring verbal and math ability, we would fit the final model to each of the two groups separately and compare. In this case, we might compare the models for males and females. We determine if the model fits equally well for each group and if the model has all of the same characteristics. The details of this are beyond the scope of this book.

To summarize, first, CFA develops a model, providing evidence that our test is measuring what we think it measures. Second, CFA examines if this model is the same for the different groups of examinees. When there is no significant difference, we have established construct equivalence or measurement invariance. CFA does all of this using the covariance among the items. Conceptually, covariance is conceptually similar to the best fitting line in regression. If items covary together, then they are highly similar and are related. When there is high covariance between the two items, examinees who do well on one item will likely do well on the second item.

4.3 Summary

It is fairly safe to assume that any large professionally developed test has been examined for measurement equivalence. Even with large professionally developed tests, these types of analyses are often hard to do because of sample size, cost, etc. For many smaller tests, it is often impractical, too costly, or just impossible to closely examine measurement equivalence (at the level most psychometricians would like). That is unfortunate, because measurement invariance is key to an accurate measurement.

Very few people even think about how the items on a test interrelate. These types of analyses are generally only understood by measurement experts. That is because the technical procedures are assessable only to highly skilled individuals. However, the ideas behind measurement invariance are not that complicated. It is just that much of what has been written on the topic misses the middle ground, making the topic assessable. Discussions tend to be overly simplistic or overly technical. This is too bad because serious conversations about test bias require an understanding measurement invariance. While this chapter certainly will not make any reader an expert, hopefully it will provide some knowledge and tools to cut through a lot of simplistic notions about test bias. Likewise, hopefully this chapter will provide enough knowledge to cut through some of the extremely technical and complicated discussions of test bias.

Discussion Questions

1. What is a psychological construct? Provide examples. Why is it hard to measure psychological constructs?
2. Explain why differential prediction is called an external approach to test bias and measurement variance is called an internal approach to test bias.
3. Describe the basic logic behind the measurement variance approach to bias. Create two matrices of graphs for a hypothetical three-item test that shows measurement invariance for one of the test items.
4. Suppose you have a test that has been shown to have construct ability in the USA, but your employer now wants to use it in Mexico. Why would it be dangerous to assume that it would show construct validity in Mexico? Describe how you would go about determining if there was measurement variance in the test between Mexico and the USA.
5. What is confirmatory factor analysis? Explain how it can be used to assess construct validity and measurement variance.

Differential Item Functioning

Contents

T. A. Stetz, *Test Bias in Employment Selection Testing*, Classroom Companion: Business,
https://doi.org/10.1007/978-3-030-89925-7_5

Objectives

- Describe the difference between differential prediction and differential item functioning.
- Explain item characteristic curves (ICCs).
- List and describe the three ways that ICCs can differ.
- Explain the statistical approach to DIF.
- Summarize research that examines DIF in standardized testing.

This chapter covers differential item functioning or DIF for short. The concepts presented in the two previous chapters will prove useful here. There are many statistical methods to examine DIF. We will only discuss one. That method is item response theory (IRT). The reason for selecting IRT is that, while mathematically it can be somewhat challenging, it is quite elegant and lends itself well to visual displays. Therefore, we can again use graphs to conceptually understand both IRT and DIF and not deal with the mathematical details. IRT has also been shown to be one of the better, if not the best, method to detect DIF and is the psychometrician's default approach for DIF analysis.

Notice that the *D* in DIF stands for differential. We have used that word before in ► Chap. 2 on differential prediction. Recall that differential prediction determines if an entire test predicts an outcome differently for subgroups. We can apply the same basic concept with individual test items. We will look at each item within a test to see if the item functions differently for different groups of people.

With differential prediction, the total test score was on the horizontal or *x*-axis, and the criterion (or what we are predicting) was on the vertical or y-axis. With DIF, a measure of ability goes on the horizontal axis, and the probability of answering the question correctly goes on the vertical axis. Thus, with differential prediction, we have a single graph for the entire test. With DIF, we have many graphs. In fact, we have a graph for each test question. ◘ Figure 5.1 shows the differences in the two approaches.

5.1 Item Response Theory Basics

Rather than a straight best fitting line, IRT uses an *item characteristic curve* (ICC) that describes how an item functions. Given the nature of IRT and ICCs, I believe examples provide the best way to understand what IRT and ICCs are all about. Suppose we give 1000 people a 10-item spelling test. We identify the horizontal, or *x*-axis, as the total test score and the vertical y-axis as the percent of people correctly answering the question. Once we have the basic graph setup, we can begin to place points within it.

◘ Figure 5.2 show this basic graph setup with three triangles plotted for the first test item. Look at the top right corner of the graph. This black triangle represents everyone who achieved a 100% on the test. They answered every question correctly and, therefore, must have answered the first question correctly. Now think about the other extreme. A score of zero. The white triangle represents everyone

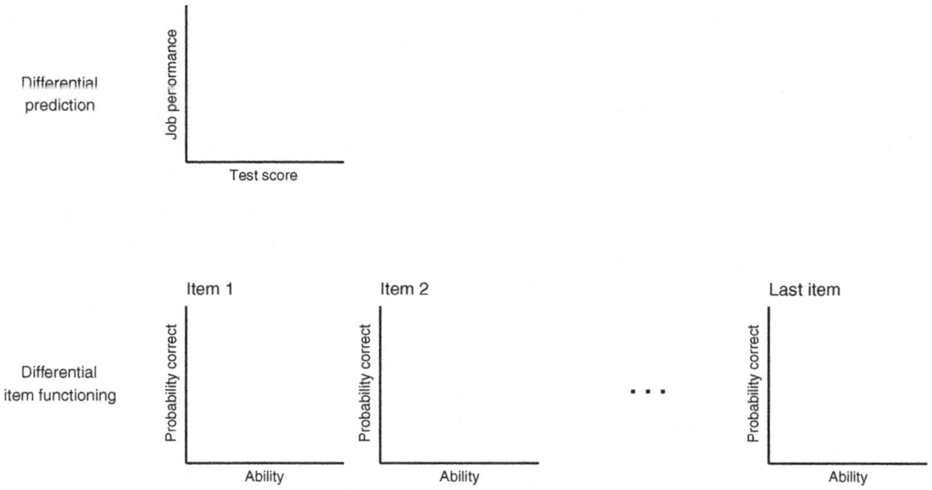

Fig. 5.1 Comparison of graphs required for the differential prediction approach and the differential item functioning approach to test bias

Fig. 5.2 Graph showing test score plotted against percent of examinees correctly answering a question

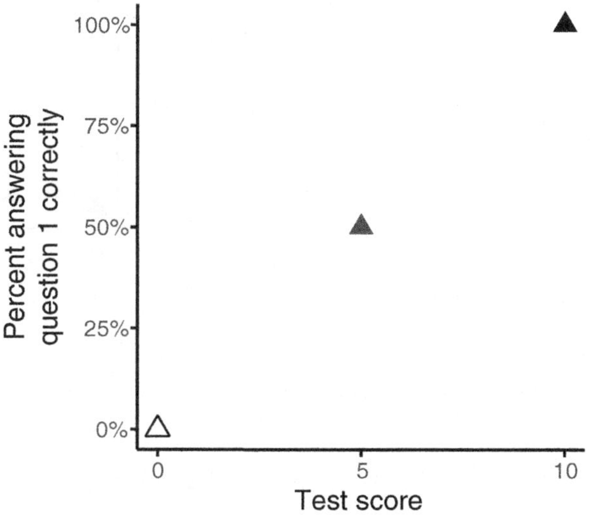

who received a zero on the test. They answered all of the questions incorrectly, and, thus, every examinee must have answered this question wrongly. Finally, consider the people who scored 50% on the test, represented by the grey triangle. They got half of the questions correctly and half of the questions incorrectly. Based on chance, most likely about half of them got this question wrongly and about half got this question correctly.

Please notice that I am using triangles rather than circles. I am doing this because in the past we have used circles to represent individual examinees. Here, triangles represented a group of examinees, all with the same score. So far, in our graph we have only included the middle group and the two extreme groups of scores. We can continue to fill in the rest of the graph. Big studies show that most likely when you graph all the possible scores, you will get a pattern that looks somewhat like an *S* in ◘ Fig. 5.3.

In the previous chapters, we fitted lines to our data and we will do it again for DIF. The dashed line shown in ◘ Fig. 5.4 is the regression line for this data. Of course, we know this is the best fitting *straight* line through the data points. However, notice that the line seems to be too high in some areas and too low in other areas. To get the line to fit the data better, we would need to make it curve. Fortunately, there is a statistical approach that will do this, and it is based on a logistic regression model. Again, the details of logistical regression are beyond the

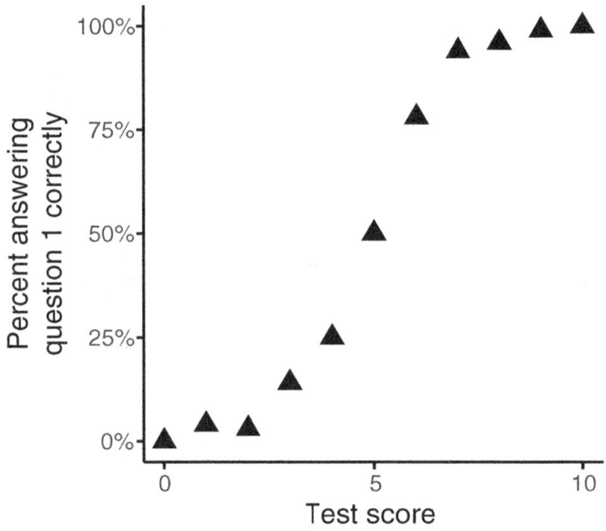

◘ **Fig. 5.3** Graph showing all possible test scores plotted against the percent of examinees correctly answering a question

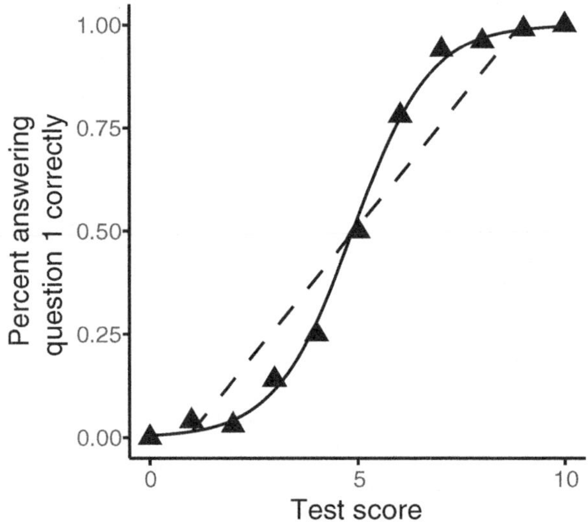

◘ **Fig. 5.4** Graph comparing linear regression line and Item Response Theory curve fitted to data points

scope of this book, but the underlying ideas are not. IRT uses this approach to fit a line that curves to the data. The solid line in ◘ Fig. 5.4 is the IRT best fitting line. Much like regression, it minimizes the amount of error in prediction. It fits the data noticeably better and is more accurate. Because it is more accurate, we should use this model over the straight line model.

Now I am going to change the labels on the graphs. First, IRT does not use the total test score on the x-axis. Instead, it uses an *ability estimate* represented by the Greek letter theta (θ). It is related to the total test score, but it is a slightly different. (Again, details that we will not worry about.) Rather than from 0 to 10 (as in our hypothetical test example above), ability estimates always the range from −4 to +4. Scale changes are common in psychometrics; however, they generally do not change things much. Consider temperature which can be measured in Celsius or Fahrenheit. The scale is pretty much arbitrary. We could use either one, and it would not change the actual temperature. We just need to remember what scale we are using.

The second label change on the graph is on the y-axis. Here, rather than the percent of examinees answering the question correctly, we use the probability of correctly answering the test item represented by $P(\theta)$. Again, this is no big deal because we simple use a scale of 0–1.00 instead of 0–100%. ◘ Figure 5.5 shows the basic features of an ICC coordinate or graphing system.

It is important to realize that different test questions have different curves. In other words, test items function differently and have different characteristics, hence the words *item*, *characteristic*, and *curve*. This is important and will play into the entire concept of DIF.

Look at the two curves in ◘ Fig. 5.6. Notice that the dashed curve is shifted to the left and the solid curve is shifted to the right. Other than this difference, they are the same. The shifting is along the x-axis and remember that the x-axis is the ability axis. Which test question is harder – the question represented by the solid curve or the question represented by the dashed curve? In IRT, psychometricians typically look at the ability level that is associated with a 0.50 probability of correctly answering the question to determine the difficulty of an item. This is the ability level where an examinee will have a 50–50 chance of answering the question

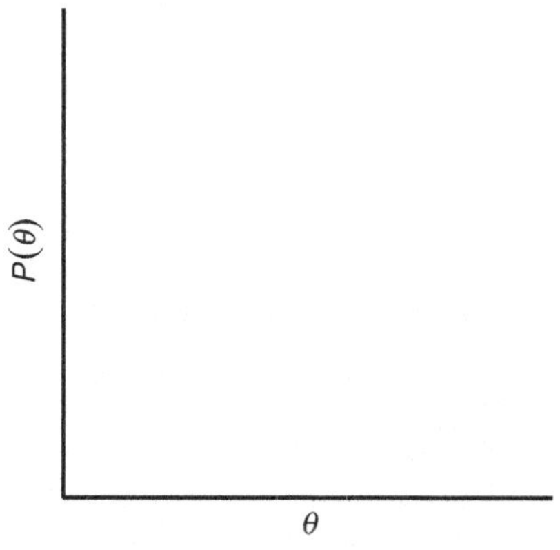

◘ **Fig. 5.5** Basic graphing coordinate system used in Item Response Theory

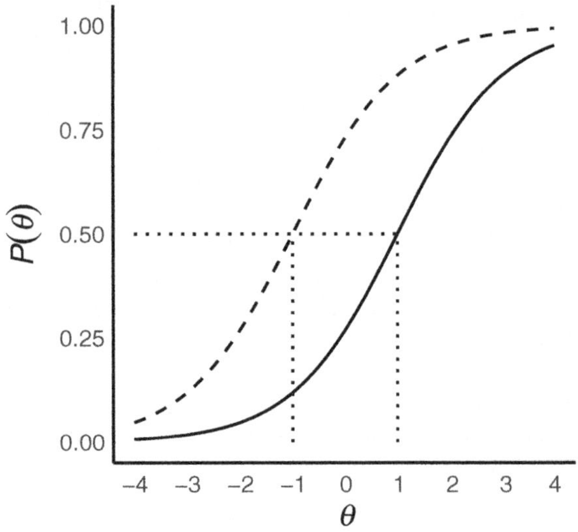

■ **Fig. 5.6** Graph showing two item characteristic curves with different difficulty levels

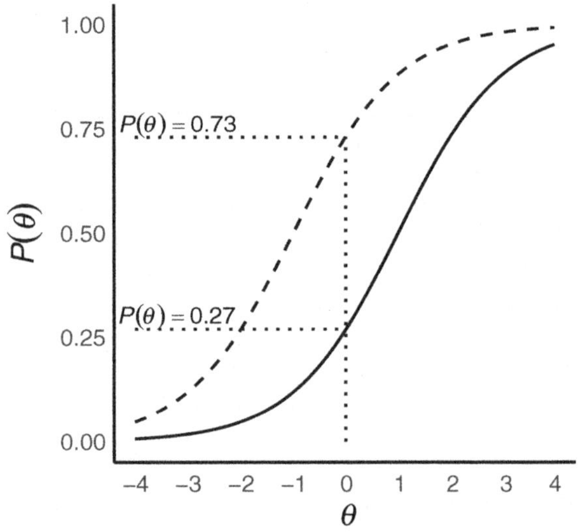

■ **Fig. 5.7** Graph showing two item characteristic curves with different levels of difficulty

5

correctly. Therefore, I draw a dotted line across the graph at $P(\theta) = 0.50$. Next, when the dotted line touches the ICC, I drop another dotted line down to the ability axis. For the dashed test question, an individual with an ability of −1.00 has a 0.50 probability of answering the question correctly. For the solid test question, an individual with an ability of 1.00 has a 0.50 probability of answering the question correctly. The solid question requires a higher ability level to have a 50–50 shot at getting it right, so it is the harder test question.

■ Figure 5.7 shows another way to conceptualize the difficulty of each question. We will consider people who have the same ability level, namely, average people right in the middle with an ability of 0.00. From $\theta = 0.00$, I draw a vertical line

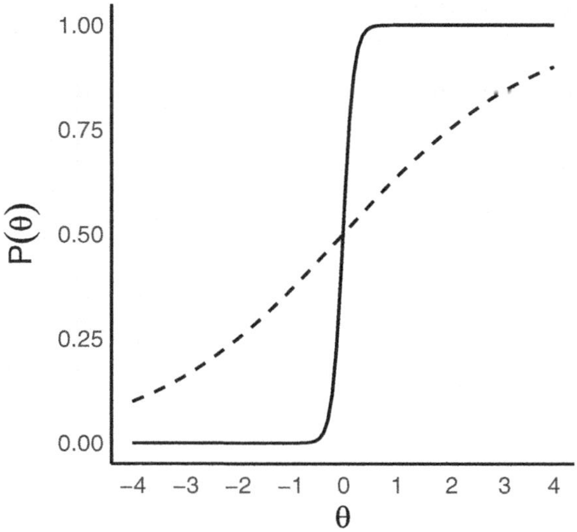

Fig. 5.8 Graph showing item characteristic curves with different levels of discrimination

up to both ICCs. Where the vertical line crosses the curves, I draw a line to the *y*-axis, showing the probability of answering the question correctly. Now we can see that a person with an ability level of 0.00 has a probability of 0.73 of answering the dashed question correctly but only a probability of 0.27 of answering the solid question correctly. Thus, the solid question is much harder than the dashed, because at the same ability level, there is a much less chance of getting the question correctly. This is how IRT determines item difficulty and is the first way that items can differ.

There are two more ways that IRT permits the items to differ. Look at the two items in Fig. 5.8. Even though they have the same difficulty ($\theta = 0.00$ when $P(\theta) = 0.50$), they look very different. The solid curve is very steep, while the dashed curve is fairly flat. How these two ICCs differ is on something called discrimination.

Discrimination may be a little harder to understand than item difficulty. The solid curve cuts the test scores sharply in half. Those with an ability level below 0.00 are almost sure to get the question wrongly, and those with an ability level above 0.00 are almost sure to get the question correct. Look at Fig. 5.9. The vertical dotted vertical lines are at ability levels −0.65 and +0.65. A person with an ability score of −0.65 has a 0.00 probability of answering the solid question correctly. In addition, a person with an ability score of 0.65 has a probability of 1.00 of answering the question correctly. Psychometricians would say that this item discriminates well, because it clearly shows who does and who does not have the knowledge to correctly answer the question. For the solid item, above 0.65 everyone is successful, and below −0.65 everyone is unsuccessful, and there is a group in the middle where it could go either way. Thus, the solid item is very precise.

In contrast, the dashed item's ICC is much flatter. It really does not cut the scores into two clear ability groups. Individuals who scored −0.65 have a 0.40 probability of answering the question correctly. Those with a score of 0.65 have a probably of about 0.58 in answering the question correctly. With the dashed item, based

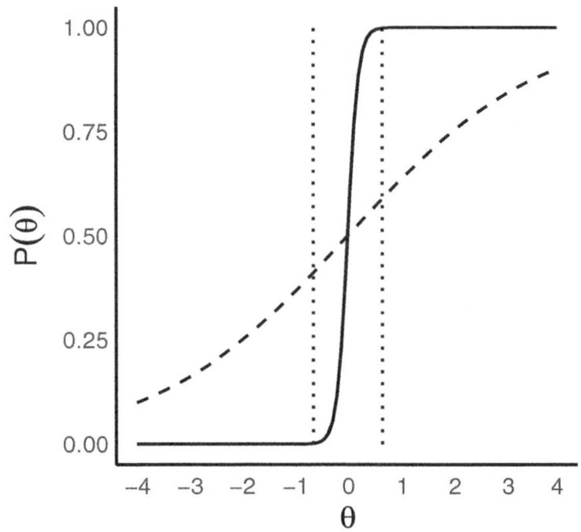

Fig. 5.9 Graph showing two item characteristic curves showing different levels of descrimination

5

on ability level, we cannot predict very well if the person will be able to get the item correct. This is in stark contrast to the solid item, where we are much more confident in our knowledge of success or failure on the item. Hence, the solid item has high discrimination, and the dashed item has low discrimination. The key point here is the steeper the slope or angle of the line, the better the item discriminates between those who know and those who do not know.

Consider this example. A test is measuring emergency medical technicians' (EMT) knowledge of CPR. With the solid item from Fig. 5.9, we can see that a person with an ability level below −0.65 definitely will not get the answer correctly. As a result, we can confidently state that this person does not have that particular CPR knowledge. Now consider the dashed item. We cannot confidently state that a person of any ability level will get the item right (or wrong). Therefore, we do not really know if the person has the required knowledge or not. As a test developer (and as a potential patient of the EMT), I would want to use the solid item. I want to know for sure that the item clearly determines if a person has the required knowledge. A very steep line like the solid item clearly discriminates if a person can get the item correct. This generally is a good thing.

The final way that items can differ is called guessing. Everyone reading this has taken a multiple-choice test. What do you do if you do not know the answer to a question? You guess. At least you will have some chance to get the question correctly. If there are four answer options, you have a 0.25 probability of guessing correctly. It is unlikely that your guess would be completely random. Often you might have enough knowledge to eliminate one or two of the options. If you can eliminate one answer option, you now have a 0.33 probability of correctly guessing the answer. For some questions, guessing is a bigger factor than others, and as a result, their ICCs will be different. If you look back at Figs. 5.8 and 5.9, you can see how guessing can affect the ICCs. The dashed ICC does not come close to the x-axis. This means that guessing is playing a role. Even a person with an ability level of −4.00 has about a 0.10 probability of getting the question correctly. The solid line is quite different. If you have an ability level of −4.00, you have no chance of getting the question correctly. You cannot even guess right. Using guessing is a little controversial in the psychometric community, but it is more often than not still used.

If we compare IRT to regression and differential prediction, we can see that there are a lot of similarities. Both approaches fit a line through our data points. These lines have properties that we are concerned with. For regression, we were interested in the slope and y-intercept of the line. In IRT, we will be interested in the difficulty, discrimination, and guessing characteristics.

► Example 5.1 No or Little DIF Based on Item Difficulty

To examine DIF, we can use an approach similar to what we used in ► Chap. 2. We create a graph that has an ICC for each subgroup. Because different statistical techniques have different historical roots, it is common for them to use different language. It is often said that statistics is a language and that you must learn the language. This is particularly true if you want to understand test bias. DIF analysis uses the words focal and reference groups. In DIF analysis, the reference group is most likely the majority group and the focal group the minority group. However, that does not have to be the case. We could be comparing different occupational groups to determine if across occupations incumbents interpret job tasks the same way. To complicate the matter more, consider the case of white females. In one analysis, white females could be considered members of the reference group if the analysis is examining racial categories (White vs. African American). In another analysis, white females could be considered members of the focal group (male vs. female).

Using a DIF model, our job is to figure out if the reference and focal groups have different ICCs. This is the same approach we used with differential prediction. If the best fitting lines for both subgroups were the same, then there was no differential prediction. ◘ Figure 5.10 shows our first graph to examine.

The graph in ◘ Fig. 5.10 illustrates a situation where there is very little DIF. In actual testing situations, it is highly unlikely that the lines will ever be exactly the same. Because these lines are so close, we would likely decide that DIF is not a significant problem with this item. One common way to examine the amount of DIF for an item is to calculate the area between the two curves. This involves some calculus and we will not get into that. The area between the two curves is very small and highlighted in grey. ◄

► Example 5.2 Significant DIF Based on Item Difficulty

◘ Figure 5.11 shows a DIF analysis, where the item displays bias based on item difficulty. There is substantial area between the ICCs for the solid and dashed groups. In this case, there is bias favoring the solid group and hurting the dashed group. Looking at an average ability level of 0.00 we can see for solid group members, there is a 0.68 probability of answering the question correctly. For the dashed group, there is only a 0.38 probability of answering the question correctly. Thus, for equal ability individuals, the question is much harder for the dashed group members than it is for the solid group

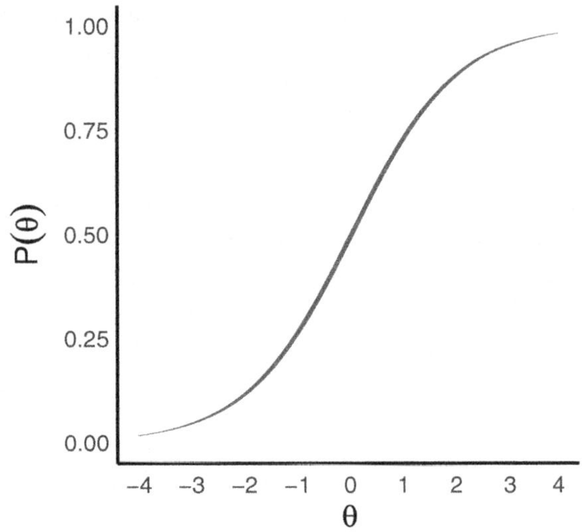

Fig. 5.10 Graph for Example 5.1 showing little to no bias

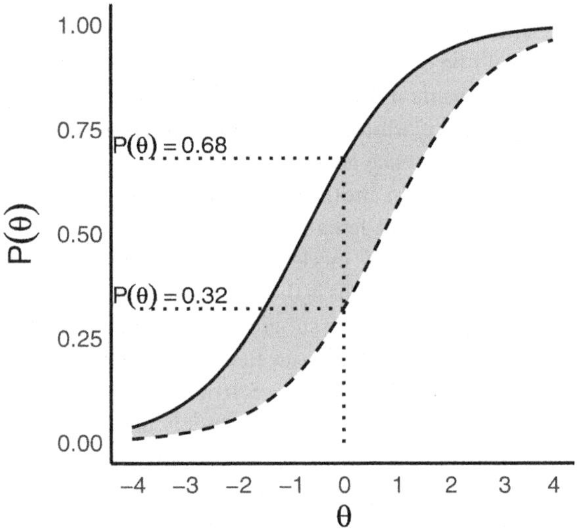

Fig. 5.11 Graph for Example 5.2 showing differential item functioning (bias) related to item difficulty

members. In the language of DIF, if the solid group is the referent group and the dashed group is the focal group, then this item would be hurting minority group members. The item would be closely examined to try to understand why it is functioning differently for the two groups and would likely be removed from the test. ◄

► Example 5.3 DIF Based on Item Discrimination

Figure 5.12 shows item discrimination DIF. In this example, the item difficulty is the same for both groups. At an ability level of 0.00, both groups have a 0.50 probability of answering the question correctly. However, at ability levels greater than 0.00, the item

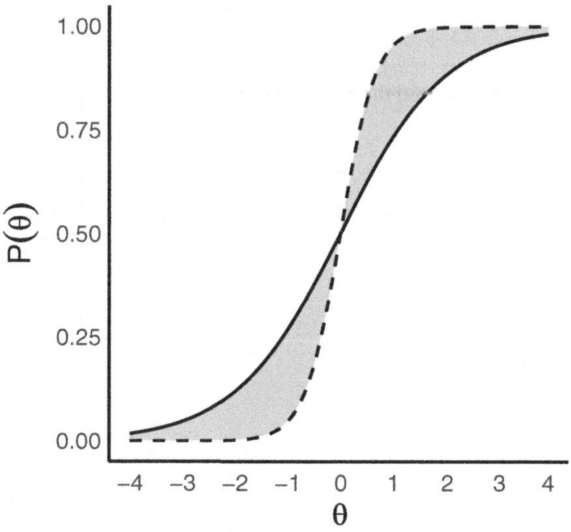

Fig. 5.12 Graph for Example 5.3 showing differential item functioning (bias) related to item discrimination

is easier for the dashed group and harder for the solid group. At ability levels less than 0.00, it is reversed. The item is easier for the solid group and harder for the dashed group. Earlier it was shown that the steepness of the ICC is related to how well the item discriminates between examinees who know the information and those who do not. In this example, the item discriminates better for the dashed group than it does for the solid group.

If we figured out the amount of area it hurts or helps either of the groups, the overall effect would be zero. The item's characteristics hurts the lower scoring dashed individuals as much as it helps the higher scoring solid individuals. For this reason, we typically do not look at the particular advantage of disadvantage to the groups. Instead, we look at the total area between the lines. We are mostly concerned with the fact that this is not operating the same for the two groups. When an item is operating differently, this is an indication of some sort of problem. We do not know what the problem is. We only know that it is not operating as we would expect and like. Therefore, it is safest to remove the item from further test use. Luckily, large-scale testing problems pretest items before they are used in high-stakes decisions, so items showing DIF are unlikely appear in tests. ◄

► Example 5.4 DIF Based on Difficulty and Discrimination

Figure 5.13 shows an example of DIF when the ICCs differ in both difficulty and discrimination. In this example, when considering individuals with an ability level greater than −1.5, the item is easier for the dashed group members than it is for the solid group members. However, when considering low scoring individuals, those below −1.5 in ability, the test is easier for the solid group members than it is for the dashed group members. Again, we do not know why this is the case. The best we can do at this point is to remove the question from the test and only use questions that operate similarly for both groups. ◄

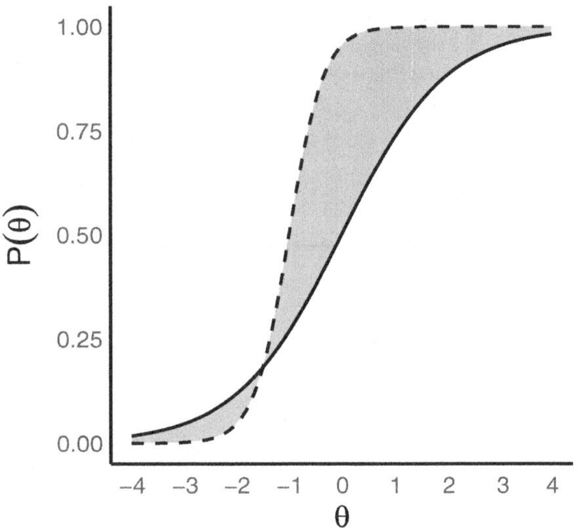

Fig. 5.13 Graph for Example 5.4 showing differential item function (bias) related to item difficulty and discrimination

5.2 Statistical Approach to DIF

The identification of test bias or DIF is not based on graphs. Graphs are helpful for understanding what is going on, but psychometrics is based on statistics. It is a number's game. As with differential prediction and measurement variance, DIF involves statistical tests. Earlier in this chapter, it was presented that ICCs can vary in three different ways – difficulty level, discrimination, and guessing. As there is an equation for regression lines, there is also an equation for ICCs.

$$p_i(\theta) = c_i + \frac{1-c_i}{1+e^{-a_i(\theta-b_i)}}$$

There is a lot going on in this equation. In statistics, we estimate things called parameters. In linear regression, we talked about the slop and intercept of the lines, which are parameters. In IRT, the parameters for the ICC are difficulty, discrimination, and guessing. When you change these parameters, it changes the way the lines look. Thus, if the groups have different lines, it is because the groups have different estimated parameters. In the above equation, difficulty is represented by b, discrimination is represented by a, and guessing is represented by c. Notice above that I used the word estimate. In statistics, we are always estimating. We could be off simply because of random chance factors. Thus, if our parameters are just a little different, we cannot really be sure that it is not just because of chance. Psychometricians by nature are a conservative bunch, which means they rather play it safe than speculate and be wrong. If there is no strong compelling evidence, they do not make strong statements, such as there is a definite difference between groups.

Statistical tests are used to determine if the parameter estimates are different for the reference and focal groups. If the difference among the lines exceeds a predetermined amount, we declare a statistically significant difference. When this happens, there is strong evidence that the item is functioning differently for the two groups that we are interested. As a result, we say that there is DIF. How this is done is beyond the scope of this book, but this is a peak behind the scenes on what statistically is going on in the identification of DIF using IRT and ICCs.

5.3 Research on DIF in Standardized Testing

Research into DIF on standardized testing has shown that *biased* test items tend to balance out over the entire test. Thus, any small advantage gained by one group on a test item is countered by another item with that disadvantages that same group. Furthermore, when items are removed, there is little impact on test scores. One of the hitches with using DIF is that it is an "internal" approach. What this means is that the ability estimate (θ) is based on the total test score. A person's performance on the test is basically used to predict how they will perform on any item within that same test. Statisticians would call this ipsative. I think the simple word circular works just as well. This type of circular measurement can create interesting situations. For example, if each and every item on a test is biased, then overall there will be little DIF. In fact, at times, the non-biased items could be the only items displaying DIF, because they are the ones acting differently.

Another interesting finding from the DIF research is that when the subject matter and test development experts are presented with the items, they are unable to identify which items will be biased and which items will not be biased. To overcome this limitation, test developers have instead implemented sensitivity reviews, which remove items that may be offensive or upsetting to examinees. However, the results of these reviews again appear to be unrelated to the actual DIF. It seems that experts cannot identify the items beforehand or later explain why an item displayed DIF. Thus, little insight is gained into why an item is biased based on a DIF analysis. Furthermore, blindly removing test items can mess up the test blueprint, which is carefully constructed to ensure the correct content coverage as well as other important testing considerations.

Most applications of DIF analysis use broad racial or ethnic groupings. Doing so results in the same problem we had with other methods. These groupings are probably only a weak surrogate for the underlying cause of bias, which is most likely socioeconomic, educational, etc. in nature. Racial groups are convenient and easy to measure, and at times you can be required to examine them, but they are not the cause of the differences. Unfortunately, when racial group differences do occur, some racist individuals take this as a support for their racist beliefs. In addition, when racial group differences emerge, some non-racist individuals become uncomfortable with the finding and blame the test as being biased. This is too bad because they focus their attention on the test, which can distract attention from the underlying causes. The test is simple an easy target. Of course, there are bad tests out there. Legitimate testing professionals go to a great deal of effort to ensure that their tests are accurate and unbiased. I can unequivocally state that testing professional want completely fair and unbiased tests.

Based on all of these limitations, is DIF completely unnecessary? Not entirely. Careful examination of test results is always a good thing. In addition, test development standards call for such analyses. However, perhaps the most important benefit is that it increases the perception of fairness. A well-accepted test must not only be unbiased; it must be *perceived* as unbiased (regardless of actual results). Whether DIF analysis results in a less biased test is an open question. But then again, as was mentioned in the opening of this book, bias is often in the eye of the beholder, because of the various approaches to bias that are not statistical in nature.

5.4 Summary

Technically, DIF is a type of measurement variance, so the material presented here could have been included in ► Chap. 4. The logic and techniques presented in the two chapters, however, are conceptually and historically distinct. For this reason, I believe that DIF should stand alone on its own. The key objective of DIF is to identify items where individuals with the same ability level, but are in different groups, have unequal probabilities of answering correctly. It should be noted that research into the practical effects of DIF is mixed. Some DIF may be benign, but in high-stakes testing environments, differences between groups need to be taken seriously. As a result, items displaying DIF should be investigated and are often removed from further test use.

Discussion Questions

1. Describe the difference in approaches between differential prediction and differential item functioning.
2. What is an ICC? Explain the coordinate or graphing system that is used for ICCs.
3. Describe the three ways that ICCs can differ. Include illustrative graphs in your answer.
4. Explain the statistical approach to DIF. What is the equation for an ICC and what are the parameters for item difficulty, and item discrimination, and guessing?
5. Summarize research that examines DIF in standardized testing. Why might someone say DIF in standardized testing is or is not a problem?

The 4/5ths Rule

Contents

T. A. Stetz, *Test Bias in Employment Selection Testing*, Classroom Companion: Business,
https://doi.org/10.1007/978-3-030-89925-7_6

Objectives

- Explain what are the Uniform Guidelines and why there were developed.
- Distinguish what is, and is not, an employee selection procedure according to the Uniform Guidelines.
- Explain the 4/5ths rule and provide a worked example of when the rule is violated and when it is not violated.
- Describe a situation where a test does not violate the 4/5ths rule, but there is still discrimination or test bias.

The 4/5ths rule is not a psychometric method of detecting test bias. However, for any employment testing situation it is an extremely important rule to know. To understand the 4/5ths rule you have to first know about the Uniform Guidelines on Employee Selection Procedures. This is because the 4/5ths rule comes from them. It can be unwieldy to write "the Uniform Guidelines on Employee Selection Procedures" every time I want to refer to it so I simply call it the Uniform Guidelines. It is also commonly referred to as the Guidelines or the UGESP.

6.1 Background on the Uniform Guidelines

The Uniform Guidelines is broad and the concepts it presents are varied. In addition, it only uses the word *bias* in a handful of places. However, it uses conceptually similar words such as fairness, discrimination, and adverse impact and spends considerable time covering forms of validity. Thus, even though the language is not precisely the same, the document essentially covers approaches to test bias. The Uniform Guidelines were first published in 1978 by four US federal government agencies. It is such an important document that anyone who works in the area of human resources should understand it.

It is helpful to have a little bit of historical background on the Guidelines. When the Congress enacted the Civil Rights Act of 1964, federal agencies became responsible for implementing, monitoring, and enforcing compliance with the Act. Because of this, several government agencies independently published guidelines on employee selection. Having several sets of guidelines was confusing and difficult to follow. As a result, four federal agencies that were heavily involved with the act got together and created a set of "uniform guidelines" that they could all agree upon (EEOC, 1978).

Four Agencies that wrote the Uniform Guidelines for Employee Selection Procedures are:

- Equal Employment Opportunities Commission (EEOC)
- Department of Justice
- Department of Labor
- Civil Service Commission (now the Office of Personnel Management)

The Uniform Guidelines where first published in 1978. The very next year, in 1979, the same four agencies issued a set of 93 questions and answers regarding their Uniform Guidelines (EEOC, 1979). It is interesting to note, and somewhat amusing, that the Uniform Guidelines is 16,816 words long and the questions and answers is 17,420 words long. Thus, right after they published the Uniform Guidelines, the agencies had to publish an even longer document to clarify the document that was meant to clarify how to stay on the right side of the law.

An important point to make is that the Uniform Guidelines are not law. They are not even regulations. Because of this, they of course do not carry the rule of law. Rather, as their name indicates, they are merely guidelines. They are intended to assist employers, labor organizations, employment agencies, and licensing and certification boards to comply with the requirements of federal law. While they are not law, nor are they regulations, the Supreme Court established in 1971 in the landmark Griggs v. Duke Power (1971) case, that the EEOC guidelines should be given "great deference" by the courts.

The astute reader will recognize that in 1971 the Uniform Guidelines did not even exist. This was the time period when different government agencies had their own unique guidelines. When the EEOC accepted the Uniform Guidelines in 1978, they became *their* guidelines by default; they assumed the "great deference" already established by the Supreme Court. Subsequent court decisions have affirmed this, and so the Uniform Guidelines are still given great deference.

6.2 What Is an Employee Selection Procedure?

Before you try to apply the Uniform Guidelines, you need to first understand what constitutes an "employee selection procedure." There is regular confusion about this. As you will see, the phrase is interpreted more broadly than you might expect. Section 2.B of the guidelines states the following:

> B. Employment decisions.
>
> These guidelines apply to tests and other selection procedures which are used as a basis for any employment decision. Employment decisions include but are not limited to hiring, promotion, demotion, membership (for example, in a labor organization), referral, retention, and licensing and certification, to the extent that licensing and certification may be covered by Federal equal employment opportunity law. Other selection decisions, such as selection for training or transfer, may also be considered employment decisions if they lead to any of the decisions listed above.

Many people mistakenly believe that the guidelines only apply to written tests. Even a casual reading of Sect. 2.B shows this is not the case. Under the definition above, many different types of personnel actions taken by organizations can be construed as an employment decision and are therefore subject to the Uniform Guidelines.

6.3 Adverse Impact and the 4/5ths Rule

The Uniform Guidelines conceptualize bias as adverse impact which they identify as a form of discrimination. The idea was originally laid out in the Griggs v. Duke Power decision. In this case, the Supreme Court focused on the fact that a minority group was disqualified by a selection procedure "at a substantially higher rate" than the majority group. Unfortunately, the court did not specify what a "substantially higher" disqualification rate meant. This lack of a clear standard lead to ambiguity, and it was difficult for organizations to use the Court's Griggs decision for guidance.

Fortunately, since the Uniform Guidelines were written after the Griggs decision, they addressed this problem by defining what "substantially higher" meant. According to the Uniform Guidelines in Sect. 4.D:

> A selection rate for any race, sex, or ethnic group which is less than four-fifths (4/5) (or eighty percent) of the rate for the group with the highest rate will generally be regarded by the Federal enforcement agencies as evidence of adverse impact, while a greater than four-fifths rate will generally not be regarded by Federal enforcement agencies as evidence of adverse impact.

If you are confused by this definition, so where many other people. The questions and answers that were published the following year included 22 questions dealing just with the concept of adverse impact.

► Example 6.1 4/5ths Rule

Sometimes definitions get in the way of understanding. It can be easier to understand a concept by working an example. The example below is from the questions and answers that demonstrate how adverse impact and the 4/5ths rule work. The questions and answers present a four-step process.

1. Calculate the rate of selection for each group (divide the number of persons selected from a group by the number of applicants from that group).
2. Observe which group has the highest selection rate.
3. Calculate the impact ratios, by comparing the selection rate for each group with that of the highest group (divide the selection rate for a group by the selection rate for the highest group).
4. Observe whether the selection rate for any group is substantially less (i.e., usually less than 4/5ths or 80%) than the selection rate for the highest group. If it is, then adverse impact is indicated in most circumstances.

Suppose an employer gave a selection test to 120 applicants. Of these, 80 were White and 40 were Black. Based on test results, 48 of the White applicants were hired, and 12 of the Black applicants were hired. This means that 60% (48 out of 80) of the White applicants were hired. Another way of saying the same thing is that the selection ratio of White applicants was 0.60. For the Black applicants, 12 out of 40, or 30% were hired. Therefore, the section ratio of Black applicants was 0.30.

If 30% of the Black applicants were hired and 60% of the White applicants were hired, then intuitively you can see that the selection ratio for Black applicants (0.30) is only one half of the selection ratio of the White applicants (0.60). Mathematically, we would calculate this by dividing the smaller selection ratio (0.30) by the larger ratio (0.60). When we make this calculation, we see that 0.30/0.60 = 0.50. This tells us that selection rate for Black applicants was only 50% of the rate for White applicants. Clearly, Black applicants were hired at a much lower rate than White applicants.

Table 6.1 Data for Example 1 of the 4/5ths rule

Applicants	Hired	Selection ratio
80 White	48	48/80 = 0.60 or 60%
40 Black	12	12/40 = 0.30 or 30%

Lowest selection ratio/highest selection ratio = 0.30/0.60 = 0.50 or 50%
50% < 80%; therefore; there is adverse impact

Under the Uniform Guidelines, adverse impact is indicated when one group is selected at a rate of less than 80% (or 4/5th) of the rate of another group. In our example, the Black applicants were selected at 50% of the rate for White applicants. Because 50% is less than the required 80%, the selection procedure is said to have resulted in adverse impact against Black applicants.

All of this is shown in Table 6.1.

In order that there is no adverse impact, the selection ratio for Black applicants would have been at least 80% (4/5ths) of the selection ratio for White applicants. In this example, it would be equal to (0.80 × 0.60) or 0.48. In other words, 48% of the Black applicants would have needed to been hired for there to have been no adverse impact. ◄

► Example 6.2 4/5ths Rule

For the next example, we will not put racial labels on the groups. This is because it does not matter which group has the highest or lowest selection ratio. When calculating the overall selection ratio, you do not always place the majority group on the bottom part of the fraction. While it is assumed that the majority group will often have the greatest selection ratio, this does not have to be the case. The questions and answers clearly state that if the ratio for "any" group is less than 4/5ths of ratio for "the group with the highest selection rate," then the 4/5ths rule has been violated.

In this example, we have three groups shown in Table 6.2.

With three groups, we have to compute three different "impact" ratios.

1. Compare Group A and Group B

   When comparing these two groups, we first noticed that Group A had the highest selection ratio, and we put it on the bottom. Group B then goes on the top of the fraction. We do the same for the two other impact ratios.

$$\frac{\text{Selection ratio Group B}}{\text{Selection ratio Group A}} = \frac{0.33}{0.50} = 0.66$$

2. Compare Group A and Group C

$$\frac{\text{Selection ratio Group C}}{\text{Selection ratio Group A}} = \frac{0.48}{0.50} = 0.96$$

Table 6.2 Data for Example 6.2 of the 4/5ths rule

Group	Applicants	Hired	Selection ratio
A	100	50	50/100 = 0.50
B	45	15	15/45 = 0.33
C	31	15	15/31 = 0.48

3. Compare Group B and Group C

$$\frac{\text{Selection ratio Group B}}{\text{Selection ratio Group C}} = \frac{0.33}{0.48} = 0.69$$

After doing the computations, we see that Group B was hired at a sustainably lower rate than Group A. Group B was also hired at a substantially lower rate than Group C. Both calculations involving Group B were lower than 4/5ths or 0.80. This is an indication of adverse impact. ◀

6.4 Why 4/5ths?

There is absolutely nothing special about 4/5ths. In fact, its use seems to be based on the "Goldilocks principle." Barrett (1998) describes that its inclusion in the Uniform Guidelines was based on the guidelines developed by the Technical Advisory Committee on Testing and published by the State of California Fair Employment Practice Commission (FEPC) in 1971. He recounts a discussion regarding the rule in one of the committee member's living rooms that 85% seemed too high and 75% seemed too low. Apparently 4/5ths or 80% was just right.

6.5 Other Important Considerations Related to the 4/5ths Rule

The 4/5ths rule was never intended to be a hard and fast rule. The Uniform Guidelines actually call it a "rule of thumb." It was really meant as a trigger to indicate when greater scrutiny was needed. As a practitioner, however, I do not want to be on the wrong side of the 4/5ths rule. It has become enshrined as a critical threshold, and once you go lower than 80%, you open yourself and your organization to issues and headaches.

Also, even if the 4/5ths rule has not been violated, it does not automatically mean that no discrimination has taken place. The rule merely places a numerical basis for drawing an initial inference about discrimination in the form of adverse impact. There may still be unlawful discrimination even if the rule is not violated. Thus, the 4/5ths does not imply that the guidelines approve up to 20% discrimination.

There are a lot of other technical details about adverse impact and the 4/5ths rule. Here are a few more issues for consideration.

Who is an applicant?

It depends on the specifics of the selection procedure, but in general, an applicant is a person who has followed the employer's procedure to express interest in a particular position and met the basic qualifications. A person who voluntarily withdraws from the process is no longer considered an applicant.

Should the overall (total) selection process be evaluated or can subcomponents be evaluated?

First, the overall selection process should be evaluated for adverse impact using the 4/5ths rule. If there is no adverse impact, then under most, but not all, cases, no further analysis is required. However, if the 4/5ths rule is violated, then each individual subcomponent of the process should be analyzed.

Should all calculations be made for all groups regardless of their size?

No. If the qualified applicant pool is less than 2% of the relevant labor market, then the group does not need to be included in any analyses.

Do you need to compare selection rates for subgroups such as White males, White females, Black males, and Black females, or can you just do analysis based on sex and then another on race?

There is no obligation to compare subgroups, such as White males and Black males. You are only required to make comparisons like males and females, White and Black. However, the questions and answers state that you are required to keep records, presumably to make such comparisons if later requested.

Can tests of statistical significance be used instead or in addition to the 4/5ths rule?

There is nothing in the Uniform Guidelines that says you cannot use tests of significance and other analyses, such as the one presented in earlier chapters of this book. The Uniform Guidelines states that the 4/5ths rule is practical in that it is an easy-to-use and easy-to-understand rule of thumb. Statistical tests are more complicated, are harder to explain, and can be influenced by many factors, including small and large sample sizes.

Are the guidelines and the 4/5ths rule out of date?

Time does not stand still in the area of employee selection. Our collective knowledge has grown greatly since 1978 when the Uniform Guidelines were published. Testing and employee selection are a very popular research area with literally thousands and thousands of studies published since 1978. Because of this, some have argued that the Uniform Guidelines are out of date and detriment to the field of employee selection. McDaniel, Kepes, and Banks (2011) published a focal article, and it resulted in 11 commentary articles debating the issue. There were good points all around. The Uniform Guidelines are probably out of date scientifically and treat adverse impact and group differences too simplistically. But then the guidelines were never meant to be a scientific document.

Regardless, the Uniform Guidelines are what has been used for over 40 years and have been in embedded in countless court cases. Furthermore, adverse impact or bias (call it what you like) is not just a scientific issue. There are complicated social and political issues as well that come into play. One advantage that the guidelines have is that they are a known entity and stable. There is no guarantee that a replacement would be an improvement.

6.6 Summary

This was just a simple introduction to the 4/5ths rule. There is a lot more to read and understand. There are a lot of technical writings and court cases. Some of them my make your eyes glaze over, and it might be tough to get through the readings, but knowledge of the Uniform Guidelines is important when dealing with bias and selection testing. Those who specialize in the topic are in demand. Even if you are not an expert in selection and adverse impact, it is a valuable skill to have, making you more employable. The American Institutes for Research (2013) performed a study for the Society for Human Resource Management on the state of HR education. They found that knowledge of staffing was the most valuable skill, increasing a student's marketability and employability. This was true at the undergraduate level and even truer at the graduate level.

Discussion Questions

1. What are the Uniform Guidelines? How and why were the guidelines developed?
2. In the eyes of the Uniform Guidelines, what is an employee selection procedure?
3. What is adverse impact and how did the concept arise? How does the Uniform Guidelines identify adverse impact?
4. Explain the 4/5ths rule and provide a worked example of when the rule is violated and when it is not violated.
5. Why is 4/5ths the threshold in the Uniform Guidelines and not some other fraction? If a test does not violate the 4/5ths rule, does that mean that no discrimination or test bias has taken place?

References

American Institutes for Research. (2013). Society for Human Resource Management's state of human resource education study. Arlington, VA.

Barrett, R. S. (1998). *Challenging the myths of fair employment practices*. Quorum Books/Greenwood Publishing Group.

Equal Employment Opportunity Commission (EEOC), Civil Service Commission, Department of Labor, & Department of Justice. (1978). Uniform guidelines on employee selection procedures. *Federal Register, 43*, 38290–39315.

Equal Employment Opportunity Commission, & Civil Service Commission. Department of Labor, Department of Justice. (1979). Adoption of questions and answers to clarify and provide a common interpretation of the uniform guidelines on employee selection procedures. *Federal Register, 44*, 11996–12009.

Griggs v. Duke Power Company. (1971). 401 U.S, 424.

Mcdaniel, M. A., Kepes, S., & Banks, G. C. (2011). The uniform guidelines are a detriment to the field of personnel selection. *Industrial and Organizational Psychology, 4*(4), 494–514.

Case Studies

T. A. Stetz, *Test Bias in Employment Selection Testing*, Classroom Companion: Business,
https://doi.org/10.1007/978-3-030-89925-7_7

Objectives

- Apply different conceptualizations of test bias to a variety of testing scenarios.
- Analyze testing situations to determine if test bias has occurred.
- Recommend courses of action on ways to eliminate test bias or reduce the potential impact of test bias.

This chapter contains four case studies that apply each test bias approach to a realistic scenario. These case studies can be used as individual assignments or group projects. They require more in-depth analysis and time than multiple-choice questions or discussion questions. Students should be encouraged to seek out and include additional information beyond what is included in the textbook.

Case Study 7.1: Predictive Validity

Fantastic Phones is a company that sells phones. The majority of their employees are customer service agents. Using a benchmarking study, the personnel department found that their competitors have been successful using personality assessments for selection with similar jobs. As a result, they wish to incorporate such a measure in their selection process. After reviewing research literature, they are considering the following two personality factors: achievement orientation and agreeableness, each measured by ten items.

Reluctant to simply spend money on unproven assessments, the CEO of the company asks the personnel department to demonstrate that the assessments are actually related to the important job outcomes. In response, they gave the 20-item assessment to 100 customer service agents. They also rated agent's job performance for customer service and sale volume as an agent's time is equally split between these two performance outcomes. Then, they used linear regression to establish predictive validity for each personality trait. This results in the four plots shown in ◘ Fig. 7.1.

The personnel department is preparing to present the results to the CEO. What should the personnel department tell the CEO during the briefing? At the end of the briefing, the CEO states that because of budget factors, they can only use one of the personality measures. Which assessment should the personnel department recommend and why?

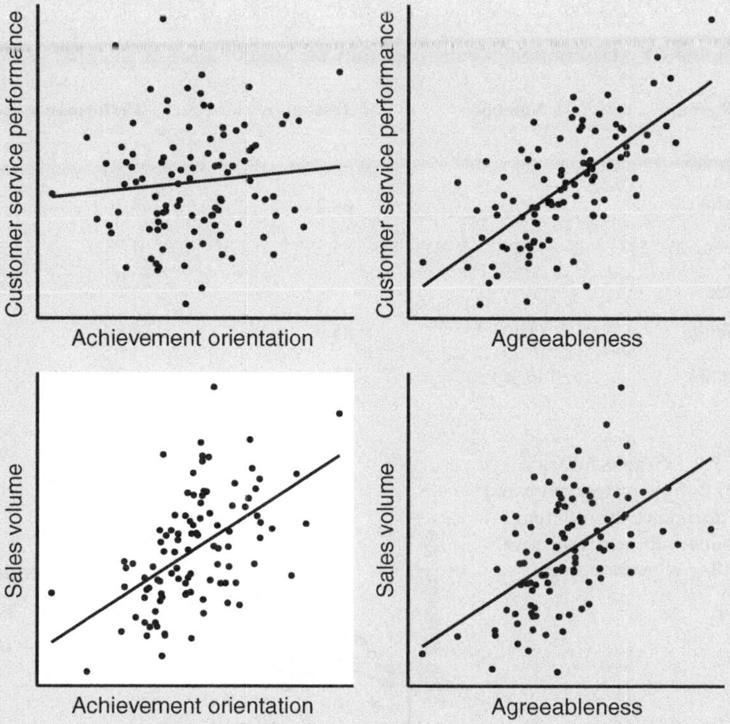

Fig. 7.1 Graphs for Case Study 7.1 showing the relationships between the predictors (Achievement Orientation and Agreeableness) and the two outcomes (Customer Service Performance and Sales Volume)

Case Study 7.2: Differential Prediction

Omni Bank is a large multinational bank. A major portion of their business is residential mortgages. As a result, they employ a large number of mortgage consultants. There is a high amount of employee turnover for the position, and they are constantly hiring new employees. Recently, the human resource (HR) office has heard complaints from line supervisors that new hires lack general knowledge about mortgages, credit, and financial information. Omni puts all new mortgage consultants through a 1-week training course on procedures and processes specific to the company, but it would take too long and be prohibitively expensive to train the new hires on this general knowledge. To solve this problem, HR contracted with a professional test development company who developed a test called the General Mortgage Information Test or G-MIT.

The G-MIT is a standardized multiple-choice test consisting of 100 questions. Although the test has several different knowledge components, only the final total test score will be used in the hiring process. To determine if the test accurately measures important knowledge, Omni gave the test to 150

Table 7.1 Description of subgroups for Case Study 7.2

Subgroup	Number	Test score	Performance score
Gender			
Male	50	68.2	7.26
Female	100	85.5	4.78
Race			
White	110	85.9	6.84
Black	40	77.5	6.28

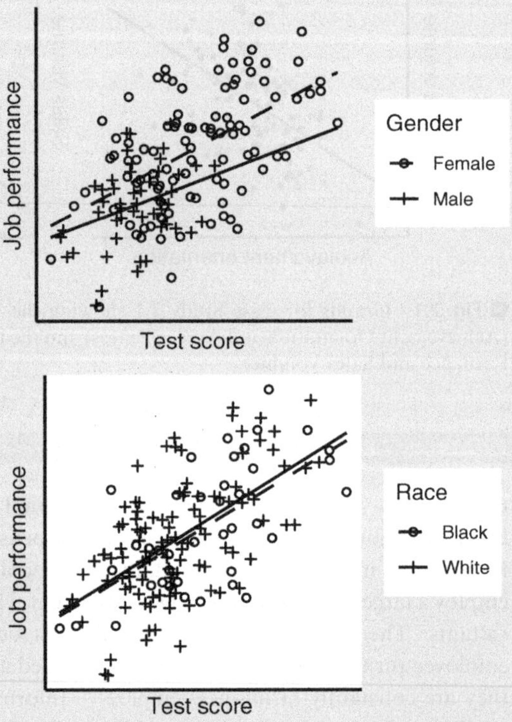

Fig. 7.2 Graphs for Case Study 7.2 showing test score and job performance for different subgroups and their respective best fitting regression lines

mortgage consultants who had been on the job for 1 year. They also collected the performance evaluation scores for these individuals. This is called concurrent validation and is a common and accepted approach to study newly developed tests in employment settings.

Table 7.1 shows the average test scores and performance scores for gender and race. Test scores could range from 0 to 100, and performance scores could range from 0 to 10. Figure 7.2 shows the scatterplots for gender and race with the best fitting multiple regression lines.

In the top panel, females are represented by white circles and the dashed regression line. Males are represented by "+" and the solid regression line. In the bottom panel, Blacks are represented by the white circles and the dashed regression line, while Whites are represented by "+" and the solid regression line.

Analyze the G-MIT results using the differential prediction model of test bias. Consider the following questions in your analysis: Is the G-MIT fair and/or biased? Is performance evaluation at Omni fair and/or biased? Is there anything Omni should further look into or be concerned about? Thoroughly explain your answers.

Case Study 7.3: Measurement Variance

The Moose Company is a multinational manufacturer of heavy duty agricultural and construction equipment. It is a Fortune 500 company and has factories in the USA, Mexico, Canada, Germany, and India. The Moose Company takes safety very seriously at their production facilities. The staffing department reviewed the research literature to locate personality traits that are associated with workplace accidents. They have determined that workers who are deliberate, agreeable, and conscientious have fewer accidents.

Being a large company, they have the resources to develop their own test. While this will cost more up front, it will save them substantial money in the long term. They followed the standard test development procedures. They first developed an assessment that consisted of 30 items equally divided between deliberateness, agreeableness, and conscientiousness. They pilot tested the items at a small factory in Iowa. From the results they selected, the five best items from each construct. The result was a 15-item assessment with five items measuring each construct. They found that the assessment was predictive of accidents (really a decrease in accidents).

Next, the Moose Company gave the personality assessment to newly hired Production Apprentices in the USA and Mexico. The assessment was professionally translated into Spanish and English, and examinees were allowed to select their primary language. This resulted in a sample of 557 assessments, of which 239 were in Mexico and 318 in the USA. ◘ Figure 7.3 shows a visual representation of the relationships among the items for the Mexican and US samples. The darker the grey, the stronger the relationship between any two items, and the lighter the grey, the weaker the relationship. Items i01 to i05 measure agreeableness. Items i06 to i10 measure conscientiousness, and items i11 to i15 measure deliberateness.

Analyze the Moose Company results using a measurement variance approach to test bias. Consider the following questions in your analysis: Is the assessment fair and/or biased? Did the assessment display measurement variance between the US and Mexican samples? If so, what actions should be taken? How should the Moose Company proceed if they wish to roll this assessment out to factories in Germany and India? Thoroughly explain your answers.

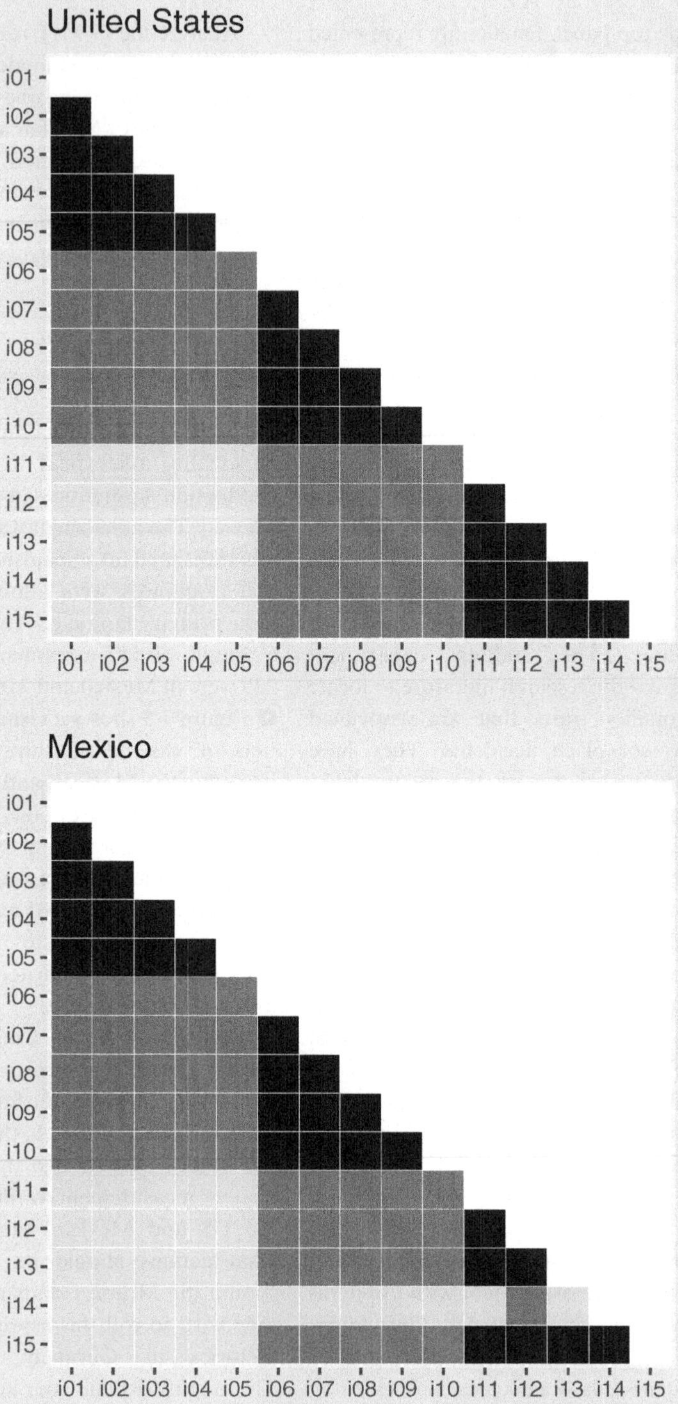

Fig. 7.3 Correlation matrices for Case Study 7.3 showing the pattern of interitem correlations for the United States and Mexico samples

Case Study 7.4: Differential Item Functioning

The Society for Measurement and Test Development (SMTD) has created a certification program. To become a certified test developer, SMTD members would need to meet educational and practical experience requirements and pass a knowledge test. The test consists of 100 questions in the following content areas: (1) history of testing, (2) norms and reliability, (3) validity, (4) legal issues, (5) tests for special populations, and (6) test bias.

During the development process, they had 50 current members take the examination. The SMTD found no indication of test bias in the form of differential prediction. In addition, they performed a differential item functioning (DIF) analysis using the item characteristic curves (ICCs). For this analysis, they also found no indication of test bias. The SMTD, however, realized that the sample during development was relatively small in size. After administration of the test to 500 certification applicants, they decided to perform these analyses a second time.

For this second larger sample, the SMTD found no indication of differential prediction test bias. They have now moved on to examine the internal functioning of the test using DIF and ICCs. ◘ Figures 7.4 and 7.5 shows the results for the five items that assess the knowledge of legal issues.

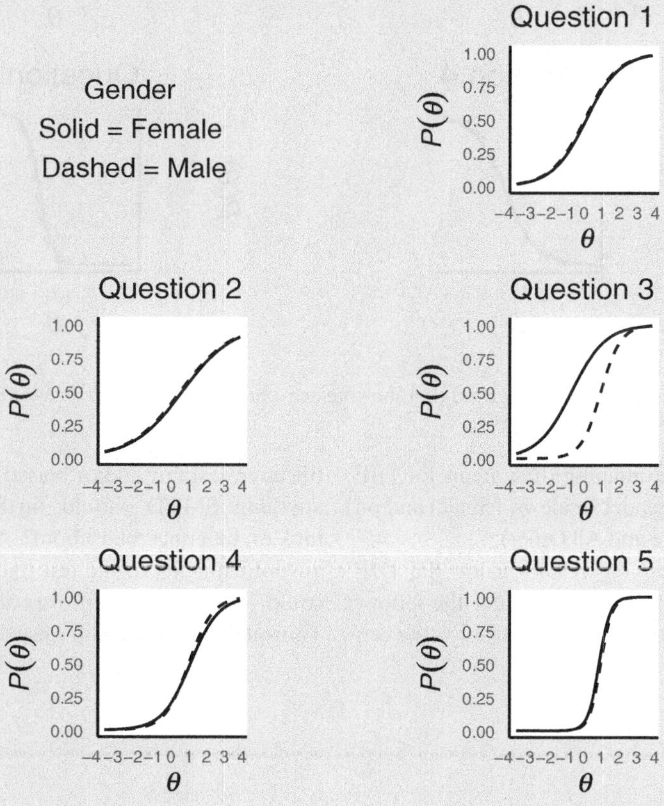

◘ **Fig. 7.4** Graphs for Case Study 7.4 showing the item characteristic curves for males and females for five test items

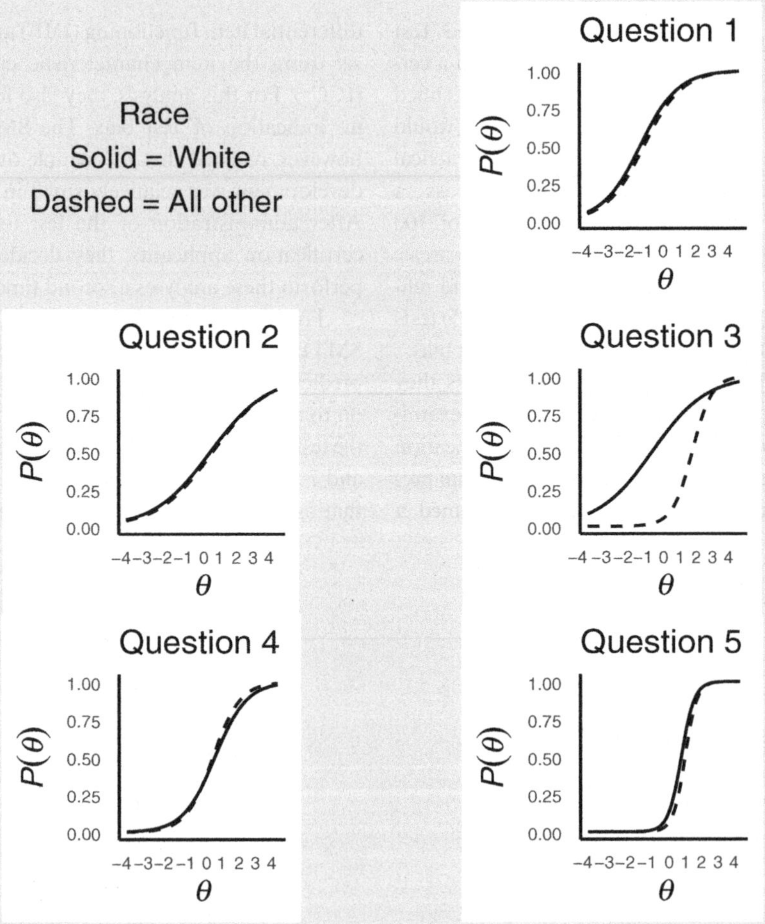

Fig. 7.5 Graphs for Case Study 7.4 showing item characteristic curves for White and All Other races for five test items

They are examining these items for DIF based on gender (male vs. female) and on race (White and All Other).

Analyze the results using the DIF model of test bias. Consider the following questions in your analysis: Is the certification test fair and/or biased? Is there anything SMTD should further look into or be concerned about? Are there any adjustments to the test that SMTD could make to improve the test? Thoroughly explain your answers.

Case Study 7.5: 4/5ths Rule

Ace Playing Card Company has recently received two new casino clients and is expanding their production operations. The company wishes to hire 11 printing assistants. The job requires that the employee first identify the correct paper to be used, load paper rolls onto the press, and set up the press. The employee then is responsible for operating and monitoring the print run. Finally, the employee performs routine maintenance on the press. The job requires strong mechanical aptitude, experience working with printing presses, and the ability to lift 75 pounds. The hiring procedure involves several steps, including a demonstration that the applicant can lift 75 pounds.

Even though the requirement to lift 75 pounds was established by a consultant specializing in setting physical requirements for jobs, the human resource department is concerned that the requirement may result in adverse impact for female applicants. As a result, after the hiring process is completed, they examine the number of applicants and hires to determine if they have violated the 4/5ths rule. ◘ Table 7.2 shows the number of applicants at each stage of the process.

Did Ace Playing Card Company violate the 4/5ths rule? Fully explain why or why not.

◘ **Table 7.2** Description of printing assistant applicants

Gender	Initial applicants	Voluntarily withdrew	Could not lift 75 pounds	Hired
Male	35	0	1	9
Female	12	1	2	2

Supplementary Information

T. A. Stetz, *Test Bias in Employment Selection Testing*, Classroom Companion: Business,
https://doi.org/10.1007/978-3-030-89925-7

Glossary

4/5ths Rule - A rule described in the *Uniform Guidelines on Employee Selection Procedures* that shows if groups have substantially different selection ratios and is used to identify when discrimination or bias has likely occurred.

Adverse Impact - A concept described in *Uniform Guidelines on Employee Selection Procedures* that describes when a selection procedure adversely affects the opportunities of a race, sex, or ethnic group for hire, transfer, promotion, retention, or other employment decision.

Best Fitting Line - A line between points in a scatterplot. In linear regression, this line minimizes the vertical distance between the line and all of the points in the scatterplot.

Bias - A technical psychometric concept that refers to systematic errors in test scores that differentially affect the performance of different groups of test takers.

Confirmatory Factor Analysis - A statistical technique that examines the relationships among test items to determine if the relationships are consistent with the intended construct.

Construct - An underlying trait, characteristic, or aspect of a person that cannot be directly observed but is instead inferred by measurements.

Construct Validity - The degree to which a test measures what it purports to measure based on the underlying pattern of relationships among test items.

Criterion - The outcome that a test is meant to predict. For example, the SAT is used to predict college performance. Thus, the criterion is college performance.

Differential Item Functioning - An approach used to identify biased test items often using item response theory as the statistical method. The approach determines if individuals with the same ability level but who are in different subgroups have the same probability of correctly answering a question.

Differential Prediction - A linear regression approach to identifying test bias that determines if a test predicts differently for subgroups.

Fairness - A social concept with various meanings, such as equal outcomes for different groups and equitable treatment of examinees.

Graph - A diagram or visual representation of data. With test bias, a graph often depicts the relationship between two or more variables.

Item Characteristic Curve - An often curved or s-shaped line used in item response theory that describes the relationship between the ability and the probability of correctly answering a test item.

Item Response Theory - A statistical model that describes the relationship between the test takers' ability and the probability of correctly answering a test item.

Linear Regression - A statistical model that describes the relationship between two or more variables by finding the best fitting line through a set of scores.

Measurement Variance/Invariance - A statistical property that indicates if relationships of variables within a construct are similar or dissimilar across groups of test takers. This can also be referred to as measurement equivalence or measurement inequivalence.

Predictive Validity - The degree in which test scores are related to the criterion (outcome). In testing, a strong relationship between the test scores and the criterion is desired and is an indication of high predictive validity.

Predictor - The variable from which predictions are made. For example, the SAT is used to predict college performance. Thus, the predictor is the SAT.

Regression Line - Also referred to as the best fitting line. In linear regression, this line minimizes the vertical distance between the line and all of the points in the scatterplot.

Subgroup - A distinct group of test takers. In test bias, subgroups are often based on race, gender, age, and disability, but they could be based on other factors.

Test - Any process or technique used to sample behavior or collect information.

Testing - A process or activity that first samples behaviors or collects information. Next, what is gathered in the first step is evaluated, scored, or interpreted. And third, based on the score an inference or prediction is made or conclusion is drawn.

Uniform Guidelines on Employee Selection Procedures - A set of guidelines issued by four federal government agencies, and given great deference by the courts, that help employers make fair nondiscriminatory employment decisions.

The manufacturer's authorised representative in the EU is Springer Nature Customer Service Centre GmbH, Europaplatz 3, 69115 Heidelberg, Germany. If you have any concerns regarding our products, please contact ProductSafety@springernature.com

Printed and bound by CPI Group (UK) Ltd, Croydon, CR0 4YY

30/09/2026

02225709-0001